Sales Thoughts

Selling at the Next Level

By Phil Bush

With collaboration from

Brett Boston

Cover Design: Gary Steele
www.creativenetwork.com

Published by Bush and Boston Associates

National Library of USA Cataloguing in Publication

ISBN 978-1-312-49985-0_____

Printed and bound in the USA

Sales Thoughts: Selling at the Next Level

Phil Bush

With collaboration from

Brett Boston

ISBN 978-1-312-49985-0

DEDICATION

This book is dedicated to my wonderful wife and daughter, and, the only hero I needed in my life, Lt. Colonel Ralph H. Bush.

~Phil

Contents

ACKNOWLEDGMENTS

I have enjoyed knowing so many colleagues during my sales career. I thank them all for working with me and being open to new ideas along the way. I hope everyone likes what he or she reads here. I hope that all my readers will become more successful in reaching their goals in life.

~Phil

Taking the long view is a skill worth developing and nurturing. Work with customers as if you were going to be working together for decades… and you may.

~Brett

Note to the Readers

This book was a collaborative effort of two close friends that have worked together professionally – sometime in the same company – for over three decades.

The voice you will hear as a reader is Phil's. The stories, examples, and key selling points are his too. He is being a little confrontational at times – "intense" and "laser-focused" are the words most people use to describe Phil when he is selling or talking about how to sell.

Phil's sales expertise, selling insights, and coaching skills are second to none. My contribution was to provide some of the strategy and process components, round out some of his insights and thinking in a few areas, and generally carry Phil's water over the course of writing the book.

It has been a challenging project for us both. We started the idea for the book while Phil was recovering from a serious accident; one that left him in a coma. He was going a little stir crazy during recovery and silly me offered to cheer him up and give him something to do by suggesting we do a book together.

We got off to a quick start, making pretty good progress for the first 6 months. Work, family, job changes, and life intervened along the way. We are both very busy people, each of us working on at least 15 things at the same time as part of our normal workloads. After many fits and starts, we had a first draft ready for our editor within a little over a year. After several drafts, re-writes, and lots of editing, another year had gone by.

After over two years of phone calls, emails, and occasional lunch meetings we have a book. Not a great book, but we think it is a solid effort, flaws and all.

We both hope you will find it a useful book, one that provides you with several practical insights or specific tactics that help you make more sales. More importantly for us both, we hope you find an idea or two that helps you become an even better, more successful sales person.

Sales professionals make things happen. We are a very special breed. Our best wishes to each of you in your ongoing sales career.

Brett Boston
Atlanta, Georgia
2014

INTRODUCTION TO DAILY SALES THOUGHTS

You are a Sales Professional.

What you do and how well you do it matters big time!

Your hard work feeds a lot of people. It drives the company's bottom line and assures the company's continued success. It also enhances your personal net worth.

You are the economic backbone of a sales-oriented, global economy.

You are good at sales. You are reading this because you are good. Why else? Because you want to get even better.

The facts about sales are pretty scary:

Two reliable studies (Harvard and Gallup), found that only four percent – that's right, 4% – of the sales people in the U.S. sell 94 percent of the goods and services.

Other, less dire studies indicate that 15% of all sales people are doing 70% of the selling.

Either way you look at it, most sales people are not as good as you are. And there is one major reason…. *Lack of planning!*

The number one reason 78% of all sales people fail, or fail to reach their sales objective, is a failure to plan.

This book tells you how and what to plan. It provides key points on upping your game with tips to extend your longevity as a Sales Pro.

Most sales people fail to understand that selling is a long-term investment in understanding your customers' needs and investing time in building strong Customer Relationships.

No one buys from someone they don't trust. You gain trust by demonstrating that you understand your customer's needs and particular business situation. Plus, you need to demonstrate how your product directly meets this need.

Overall, you have to demonstrate that your customers are buying more than your product; they are buying your expertise and your commitment to help them solve problems.

In short, you must be seen as a "Trusted Business Advisor" (TBA) and not "just" a sales person.

This is the key message of my book. Trusted Business Advisors (TBAs) are the top sellers in every field. They understand their customers by investing time and energy in building Customer Relationships and demonstrating capabilities beyond the product.

A couple of more industry-generated numbers may help you understand why Account Planning and building strong TBA relationships constitute THE KEY TO SUCCESS.

2% of sales are made on the first contact

3% of sales are made on the second contact

5% of sales are made on the third contact

Only 10% of sales people make more than three contacts

10% of sales are made on the fourth contact

And... get this... fully 80% of sales are made on the fifth to twelfth contact.

Think about it. The 15% of sales people making 70% of the sales are the sales people who "get it." They understand these statistics and have a plan for building relationships and establishing TBA status over a period of time.

Our goal in this book is to dramatically lift your sales game. Read on to learn how to become a Trusted Business Advisor through some basic sales planning strategies.

ONE – BECOMING A TRUSTED BUSINESS ADVISOR

First Thoughts

Great sales people are strategic listeners. They ask great in-depth questions about the customer's problems and needs. The quality of these questions demonstrates knowledge about the customer's interests.

Customers and pros view top sales people as business consultants and go-to problem solvers. This is because they do thorough meeting preparation, advanced research about the customer, and they also develop great consultative questions.

This is game-changing behavior. Learn it. Do it.

1 – Strategic Listening – A sales skill that separates good from GREAT sales professionals.

Great sales people are strategic listeners. They work hard to be viewed in a strategic light.

- They ask great in-depth questions about the customer's problems and needs.
- They demonstrate knowledge about the customer's business via the quality (not quantity) of the questions they ask.

Great sales people are focused on learning by *first* asking questions about the customer's business. This is not about using the same list of questions for every customer. It is about…

- Doing advance research.
- Determining the customer's most current list of strategic projects.
- Asking clarifying questions about those projects.

Ask enough questions to get strategic knowledge so you can explain how what you sell can help the customer BETTER achieve their Strategic Goals. In short, your motive is to help improve the customer's understanding and effectiveness by explaining their problems and needs to you.

By asking clarifying questions, you help the buyer perceive you as having a level of respect and understanding that is, unfortunately, all too rare in sales professionals today.

Sales Thought: By NOT talking about the product you sell, you will create an interested buyer.

By taking a consultative approach from the start, you lead customers to respect you and what you are trying to accomplish. In most cases, customers will want you to keep asking questions because this helps them clarify the issues they are facing for themselves. It is a unique customer that will not be happy to answer strategic questions focused on understanding of *their* business issues.

Additionally, the customer will appreciate how you link what they are trying to accomplish to what you are trying to sell. That is the nature and power of strategic listening. Strategic listening creates a genuinely interested buyer who has a great deal of respect for you, the seller.

Sales Thought: Through meeting preparation, up front research about the customer, and great consultative questions, top sales people are viewed as business consultants and go-to problem solvers by customers and prospects.

Sales Tactic: Strategic listening is a winning skill for elevating your sales game for each customer.

Example: When called upon to present a product, a sales person I worked with brought their strategic listening skills to the table. Rather than just focusing on their product, they spent considerable time learning about the customer's business. Although the sales person also had to present what they were selling, they spent most of the time listening to the customer talk about their business and business issues. This helped the sales person understand the customer's true needs.

As a result, the sales person won the deal and established a reputation with the customer for being focused on understanding true business needs and addressing them directly.

If a customer doesn't want to talk about his or her own company, this should be a warning signal to the sales person!

2 – How do you learn the "big picture" issues that are driving client decision-making?

Selling is less about what you want to sell and much more about what clients need. Today's customers are better informed and often have a very good idea of what they are looking for. The selling challenge is to map a customer's "stated" need into bigger picture issues driving their business.

Linking your product to identified "bigger picture" needs of a customer's business is a tricky proposition. Depending on what you sell, customers will state needs in terms of product specifications. Avoid taking this specification "bait!" Product specifications provide little insight into the real problems the customer is attempting to solve.

Sales Thought: Work to first understand the real business drivers facing the client. Think beyond the stated needs.

This is about not just focusing on what your client says that is currently is going on, but also about things that might be going on in the future. Referencing similar organizations that you have worked with that seem to have similar issues can be one way to check on your understanding with the client.

Depending on what you sell, the prospect may have an expectation that you will come to the first meeting not only with well thought out questions, but also suggestions on how you might apply your product to their business. After listening to some of the issue the prospect is having, and asking some probing questions to be sure you have enough understanding, a *reference story* may be a good way of summarizing your understanding and explaining to the prospect how another client handled a similar situation.

Sales Tactic: Use reference stories in your first meeting. By talking about how other organizations have used your product to address issues, the issues that your current prospect may also be experiencing. This is a good way to get things rolling at your first meeting.

Sales Thought: Identify how your product fits within the big picture needs of a customer's business.

Failure to uncover how this product fits a customer's true business drivers will greatly reduce the odds of completing the transaction in a timely manner. A customer nearly always must connect your product to at least one big picture business driver or business need for you to complete the sale.

Steps to Take:

1. At the initial customer meeting, skillful questioning based on prior research provides the basis for uncovering big picture drivers.
2. Public companies and government agencies often share strategies and major initiatives on their websites and within press releases.
3. It can be even more difficult to uncover business drivers for a private company.
4. Smart sellers use a customer's competitors as a means of research. For example, you might ask, "We understand that your competitors X and Y are both looking at approach Z. What approach are YOU taking to address the issue?"
5. Customers often like to discuss competitive challenges. When you are not sure of big picture drivers, give the customer a chance to talk about how they are handling their competitor's moves.

Example: A financial services customer of mine had a stated goal of cost reduction and indicated that they were going to reduce costs through a combination of eliminating certain facilities as well as trimming Information technology costs. Think of this in the following fashion:

We asked the Customer to indicate to us "How" they were going to do it. There are a lot of different versions of "How." This one involved getting to the heart of the matter and asking a series of questions regarding the "How" portion of the strategy.

Why does this work? Because Sales People who learn to ask educated questions typically endear themselves to the potential customer.

It does not mean you can just go in yapping about your product, but if we do a good job with the questions we ask, we can learn a tremendous amount.

In some cases, the Customer may not have always thought the matter through in that level of detail.

So, via the Q&A, we get here:

Goal: Cost Reduction

- Strategy 1: Eliminate (close) certain facilities
- Strategy 2: Reduce IT costs

Sales Tactic: I asked questions to confirm the reason they were interested in my product and services. I then asked questions regarding how they saw my product and service offering could assist with the goal of cost reduction and how we could help them achieve ether one or both of their stated strategies.

In short, I let the customer explain to me the link they saw between my products and services and their business drivers. My job was to fill in a few additional links between my products and service and their business needs.

Sales Thought: As a Sales Professional you must:

- Understand your customer's business drivers
- Link those business drivers to capabilities your product provides

Sales Tactic: True sales professionals provide a logical linkage between client needs and specific product capabilities.

Remember, selling is not about telling the customer what they need, but more about helping them make the connection between their needs and issues and your product capabilities.

3 – There are two key points to uncover in a sale: "WHO is responsible for achieving the goal within the customer's organization?" and "How urgent is it?"

Above, I talked about the financial services customer with the goal of reducing costs. Understanding the customer's business drivers, the goals, and the strategies was the first part of the sales process. Next, through effective questioning, I was able to link my products and services to the customer's business drivers.

But the link to the business drivers, while essential for making the sale, was not sufficient to ensure a speedy close. Moving the sale forward expeditiously requires an understanding of additional information about the customer's organizational dynamics. To get there …

The next step was for me to better understand WHO was responsible for achieving the goal and how URGENT achievement of the goal was to the organization.

The rest of the story was getting to the intersection of these two additional important understandings.

Sales Tactic:

1. Ask questions to determine WHO owns the goal or business driver within the organization.
   a. WHO in the organization is achievement of the goal most important?
   b. WHO is the organization holding accountable for achieving the goal?
2. How URGENT for the customer organization to resolve or achieve the goal?

Answering the WHO questions will allow you to focus your selling efforts on the right person within the customer organization. Often, the people assigned the task of dealing with you are NOT feeling the same level of importance in resolution of the goal as the WHO you identify. Taking your sales approach directly to the identified WHO will greatly improve your chances of success.

Also, understanding the URGENCY of resolving the problem or achieving the goal will provide you a sense of timing and pace for working with the customer.

Answering both of these questions -- WHO and URGENCY -- will help you understand the nature of your opportunity. Failure to answer these questions would give you an incomplete understanding of the selling landscape.

Sales Tactic: Make sure you position your sale as close as possible with the person for whom the goal is important and urgent.

It is a really sinking feeling when the person for whom the goal is important and urgent parachutes into the selling process at the final stages, just when you thought you were moving to a close. Should this happen, you can rest assured that your opportunity for a fast close will fall apart! If you are lucky, you might get to start the process over, with the opportunity to sell to the real WHO on the account. The worst case is that you are seen as not understanding the WHO's goals and URGENCY (since you have never spoken to them directly!) and therefore lose your selling credibility within the account.

4 – Sellers rarely get in trouble by asking good, well thought out questions.

If you have done the proper advance work, and you are asking questions that demonstrate your understanding of the customer's business, you are now in a great position to being positioning the capabilities of your products and services. Demonstrate how the capabilities you are discussing will help achieve part or all of the customer's goals.

Sales Thought: What experienced sales people do well, is ask questions of the Customer; questions based on prior learning and research.

Example: I regularly monitor press releases from my key customers. From a recent press release I learned a customer had indicated they planned to expand operations internationally. During my next routine follow-up call on the customer I asked 2 questions of a C-level executive at the account:

"I have been following the news of your planned international expansion.

1. Does this expansion affect your role within the company?

Turns out it did. The international expansion meant a significant increase in responsibility for this executive. She told me a great deal about her expanded role – the things she was looking forward to and some concerns.

2. What capabilities will you need in order to properly execute internationally?"

This question lead to a long discussion about existing product capabilities she had that she wanted to "export" to the overseas operations, and new capabilities she would need for the expansion. This question lead to a discussion of a product feature set that we offered, but that she was unaware of, as she had not needed it before now.

These 2 questions, based on routine research tracking, started a new and lucrative sales cycle.

Said another way, it is not always readily apparent if a customer is ready and willing to start down a new purchase path. It takes skillful questioning, based on research to uncover new business needs.

Sales Thought: Good questions can also help uncover the *real* reasoning behind why a particular capability (the product or service you are selling) is suddenly of interest to the customer.

Sales Thought: Great questions can help you uncover new needs, link your product to the customer's big picture business drivers, and help you position particular capabilities of your product as a solution.

5 – Understand the "whole" customer: Do you have a "holistic" view of your customers' business needs? Or do you just "respond" to the customer request, as presented to you?

Your position, even with your best customers, is variable and at the whim of changes within your customer's world that you don't control. New management, new business directions, new processes, and new philosophies at the account, all equal account risks. Understanding these account risks can ensure you are not just "responding" to a request, but are also providing background context for understanding the reasons behind the request.

It is important for you to learn and understand what is driving a customer's request. Think about it as a skill or technique for getting to the heart of the matter. This means that you ask specific questions that will lead to a holistic understanding of what is driving your customer to make this request, or at least to make a move in this new direction.

Think about it in these terms: requirements for a particular request for a new capability don't just invent themselves. The customer specifically makes these requests because of a direct need for these new capabilities and a desire to acquire them – but stated them as a product specification or enhancement.

However, as opposed to immediately responding to those capabilities with a "yes" or a "no", the better approach is to dig for deeper understanding of the drivers behind the request. Ask questions that will help you get to the heart of their real needs from a holistic perspective.

Sales Thought: Behind every request or requirement is a driving business reason!

Sales Tactic: Think about these questions as a way to get the "rest of the story" behind the requirements, or what may sometimes be called a business issue:

- What is driving this requirement?
- How long has this been an issue?
- If this issue has existed for a while, why do you need to address it now?
- What compelling event has caused you to go forward now with an acquisition?
- If the issue has been out there for a while, are you concerned your competitor may be addressing this business issue and you have not?

These questions should take you down a path where you have a true holistic view of your customer's business.

6 – Selling Principles do not change, no matter the era. Understanding the customer's business problem is still job one!

A lot of sellers have a difficult time focusing on their customers or prospective customers. Why? It's because they are usually trained to focus on one thing and one thing only: the product they are selling. This tends to blind sellers to what really matters. And what really matters is the customer's set of business issues.

No matter what you do, and more importantly, no matter what the era, this is a fundamental principle of selling.   If you don't understand who you are selling to and what they want to accomplish, you are simply "pitching product." In today's marketplace, this rarely works. With customer needs and company purchasing processes getting increasingly more sophisticated, the pressure is on the seller to focus on the customer FIRST.

Example: I coached a Sales Professional whose product was generally viewed by the market to be "not as good as the competition's offering." As a seller, he was taught to focus on pitching how great his company's product was and he was well-schooled in overcoming the objections for why the product was not inferior to the competition's. In this particular case he was making a call on a manufacturing company, and knew his product was not viewed favorably. The Sales Pro took my advice and decided instead to focus on first understanding the company's business issues. At the first meeting *he did not present anything*, but instead asked Strategic Questions of the buyer. He let the buying committee know he was not ready to talk about product fit until he better understood the business issues and needs of the buyer. The win in this situation was big. After he met with the buying committee, the seller found that, while they were shocked about the questions, they were very surprised that his priority was to first learn their buying Issues. This significantly impacted their view of all the other presentations from the competitors. Competing sellers talked about their products and great features. This Sales

Professional won the evaluation, and the win had little to do with a "product pitch."

Sales Thought: Buyers fully expected the seller to talk about his or her product, so this approach – first understanding the buying issues before pitching product – is an immediate game-changer.

The lesson to be learned here is that most (though not all) buyers are looking for long-term relationships with a seller and are not just purchasing a product.

Sales Tactic: Many buyers will trade-off features for a demonstrated consultative relationship with the seller.

This key selling principle will serve you well as you go about your selling career.

7 – Focusing on the ultimate goal for each account is key. Plan your engagement strategy with the end game in mind.

As you work with each customer, always keep your Plan for the account in mind. For some accounts your plan may be to just "sell the next deal" and, at many companies, that might be enough. The problem with this approach is that if you go about selling in a thoughtless, unplanned way, your customers will quickly figure out that there is no professional depth to your selling game. If all you care about is the "next deal," your customer will begin to sense that you don't actually value their business interests and needs. Again, if you can do this and be successful, far be it for me to tell you not to work this way. But, there is an alternative…

For certain sales people at certain companies, success is about building strategic relationships with customers and helping customers achieve their goals. This means focusing with the end game in mind. It doesn't need to happen every time, but it should be your focus for accounts having what you believe can represent huge long-term potential. Clearly, one of the things you have to learn to do is to pick and choose the accounts for which you will take the time to plan and implement a strategic selling approach.

Now, if you want a strategic relationship with a customer, you have to be prepared to invest to get it. Strategic relationships require an investment of time, talent and treasure. Many sales people simply can't invest in accounts, due to limited seller-side resources, or don't want to take the time to plan out a strategic sales approach. If so, perhaps you can get by without a strategic relationship.

If you are not prepared to invest, I ask you to remember a movie scene from *The Untouchables* featuring Oscar winner Sean Connery. In the movie, Connery is part of a group trying to put away Al Capone. Connery is told by a Treasury Agent that the Agent would do "anything he could" to help. Connery shot back, "But THEN what are you prepared to do?" Selling success comes from being prepared to go the extra mile by investing time, talent and treasure in the account, not just being willing to go the extra mile.

Sales Thought: *In nearly all cases*, if you are not prepared to invest, you cannot change the selling relationship to a more strategic one.

Depending on your current relationship, moving it to the next level is typically about proof - proof that you are willing do several things and likely all at the same time:

- Proof that you will invest in the relationship and not be a "hit and run" seller. Investing in the relationship means putting time effort and money into the relationship when there is nothing financially at stake – No current Deal on table! Are you prepared to make this type of Investment?
- Proof that you are interested in the customer's success, and that what you are selling will successfully address the customer's needs.
- Proof that you have a clear plan for how your product will address the customer's needs.

Demonstrating these points gives the customer assurance they will get the resources they need to be successful using or implementing your product. This concept is always a little controversial. Think of it as providing a road map that indicates to customers how they can get there with your product.

Sales Thought: Having a well thought out plan for the account demonstrates to the customer your ongoing commitment to their success.

It typically can't only be about providing a "Point" Solution. It needs to be about solving an on-going problem, helping different people in the business address Other Business Issues. It's an investment to ensure they experience broad success in the long run.

I will talk more about the critical role of account planning in the next chapter.

8 – If approached properly, selling and sales is less about "pushing product" and much more about facilitating solutions to the customer's key business issue!

In this day and age, selling continues to evolve. The sales process is much less about having a great product, and much more about **demonstrating value** to your customers. Why? Customers are much smarter and well versed in nearly all products for sale than they used to be. The amount of information available about products continues to expand almost daily.

Sales Thought: One key to be being a successful seller in this day and age is demonstrating YOUR value – as much or more than your products value. It can be the key differentiator for most sellers!

Demonstrating value has everything to do with focusing on the customer. Learning the nature of the customer's business needs will serve most sellers very well. Learning about the customer's business demonstrates that you are interested in being of value.

Sales Tactic: Most great sellers spend a minimum of 2 times the length of their scheduled meeting time with each customer in preparation mode. Preparation may include reviewing customer press releases that speak to what the customer is doing in the marketplace, job changes, new products and services, and new corporate directions.

In an initial customer meeting, you have a very limited window of time to demonstrate value. I suggest you want foremost to demonstrate so the buyer that you are a "different" breed of sales person and unlike the last twenty they interacted with. To that end, if you come in armed with knowledge about the customer's business – or at a minimum, great questions to gain knowledge about the customer's business – you have a better chance to make a positive impression.

Of course your approach will be based on what you sell. If your product is designed to help a customer with their supply chain, come to the meeting with prepared questions focused on their Supply Chain.

The information you need to prepare for the meeting can be gleaned from general sources or people you have talked to inside the company. Preparing puts you in a category of seller very different from the rest – focused on defining value for the customer, not pitching product.

Sales Thought: The more you can demonstrate value by showing your understanding of their business issues, the quicker you separate yourself in the client's eyes from mediocre sales talent.

The most important goal of a first meeting is to demonstrate your knowledge and understanding about the customer's specific needs and business issues.

Selling Tactic: Pre-develop specific, in-depth questions to ask your customer about their business plans and goals that will clearly demonstrate your in-depth knowledge and your willingness to prepare.

9 – What are you willing to invest in understanding and addressing a customer's business issues? Which accounts warrant investment in developing a long-term relationship? It's about Engagement!

If you are going to remain in sales as your life's calling, one of the key points you have to decide on is the amount of time you will spend/invest in various functions necessary to effectively do your job. You also have to develop the appropriate time allocation skills that will allow you to continue to expand your client base, as well as improve your relationships with existing customers.

Sales professionals find the right balance and right criteria by answering 2 important questions:

1. What is the right mix/balance of time to be allocated to existing customers to cultivate long-term relationships versus investing time in expanding your client base?
2. How do you decide the client's that are worth the investment of your time to establish a long-term relationship?

The most important thing to decide is what level of engagement you are going to use with each customer or potential customer. Having a formal sorting filter like the 2 questions above, is an area that often gets overlooked by sales people, but can make a big difference in ensuring you move forward with each customer with the right level of investment on your part.

Depending on what you sell, the answers in terms of investment in engagement are clearly different. The most important thing going forward is to make sure that prior to your working with a new potential customer you categorize the level of time and resource investment appropriate to the account.

Here is a list I use for determining the potential investment level warranted by a client:

- Current customer with potential to spend more money if they see the need. Large account expansion within existing customers offers the best alternative for prioritizing your limited time and resource investment.
- Long-term, high-value accounts. If you can penetrate these accounts (usually big-name player in their respective sectors), you can make a bottom-line difference for your company. These accounts have high potential value in terms of sales and reference to you and the company and are worth a high upfront investment of time and research.
- Those who work collaboratively with your company in joint marketing, product development, or sector penetrating, and will provide great references.
- New Customers based on reference selling that come to you on a reference from an existing customer. The best sales people of your product in most cases will be your current customers who think highly of you and your company.

All customers "require" a professional sales effort from you, but you must of necessity make choices in the optimum investment of your time. If times are slow, you can afford to make more substantial investments in all accounts, and should. If you are really busy, you will have to make investment choices to prioritize the best use of your time and resources.

Sales Tactic: First, seek to understand and prioritize your ability to invest in a particular customer and only then engage in selling.

10 – There is a skill in doing "enough" research to engage the client in a meaningful conversation about their business.

So how much research is enough to demonstrate that you have sufficient business knowledge about the client's business, business sector, strategic direction, or competitive marketplace? Not an easy question to answer simply, but the indicators are that you have done enough research to answer the basics:

- Company strategy
- Markets and value of the business
- Organizational structure, particularly within the client's end of the business
- Competitors
- Key products
- Read the recent press releases
- Tapped the business blogs on analyst's assessments

It is important to demonstrate to the client you are not just an expert on your own products, but you have also spent time researching the client's business and where they are headed. The conversation should be focused on understanding the "So what?" driving where the customer's business is headed. Further, you need to position how the capabilities of your products may help the client see the value your company brings to the table; value specifically related to helping the customer succeed.

You do not need to be an expert on their business, but you need to know enough to engage the client in a meaningful conversation with well formulated questions that demonstrate you did your homework and prepared for the meeting – in itself, a differentiator from sales wannabe's.

Sales Thought: If you do "enough" research to engage a customer in a meaningful business needs conversation, the selling outcome is more likely to be positive.

Example: I know when I am nailing the questions and the conversation with a new customer when the customer takes the lead to provide me additional selling insight that allows me to better position my product.

By continuing to ask well thought out questions, most potential customers will quickly determine that there is something "different about this sales person." In short, it is easy for a buyer to spot a true sales professional; they stand out in the crowd.

There is no "magic" formula to the amount of time one should spend with each customer. Sales people have to determine that for themselves, and focus their attention on developing relationships. Not every client will require or appreciate the same amount of time investment.

Sales Thought: Sales professionals plan for and invest the time to learning about their clients' businesses and business issues. Clients notice the preparation as professionalism. Viva la difference!

11 – The moment the sale is closed, the next sales cycle begins!

Sales Thought: How you handle the transition from the close of the sale to the next sales cycle is critical to setting up a long-term relationship with the client.

Clearly, the most important sales step is to ***get the initial sale completed and closed.*** Closing the Initial sale is hard work. From the close of the deal, the relationship transitions from buyer-seller to customer-account. Good sales people know that to become truly successful, it is more important to stay connected to the new customer and clearly define the long-term relationship. The best way to do this is to focus on the Big Picture and set a long-term vision for how you can assist your client going forward!

Sales Thought: Proper handling of the transition will determine if a longer-term relationship can be established between the sales person and the customer.

The sales close is a time for determining and establishing your long-term role and value to the account. Keep in mind that it is always easier to expand the sale within an existing, satisfied customer that it is to find a new one. So don't relax now, push forward and close with an exclamation mark.

The sales process should now be developed in such a fashion as to ensure and convey to the customer that there is both a short-term *and* long-term focus to the relationship.

Example: One Sales person I know had a great plan for long-term success. As he closed each Sale, he set up a social hour with the customer to thank them for their business. By doing this, the sales person set a tone for future business. This social hour became a way for the sales person to ask more questions of the customer, and the customer, being in a social setting without the pressure of the "Deal" was much more open and relaxed with the sales person.

More questions were asked and the next 3 opportunities came up in "casual" conversation.

Sales Tactic: Grab the short-term victory, while simultaneously getting the customer to look at the long-term relationship with you.

Sales professionals manage the transition.

12 – Starting the next sales cycle with an existing customer.

So you want to be around for the next sales cycle, eh? Well there are a 2 key things you can at the close of the first sales cycle to better position yourself for the next sale within this new account:

1. Make sure you have done your homework and demonstrated you understand the customer's existing and evolving business issues.
2. Ensure you help the customer understand how you can help them address their current need AND longer-term needs.

Utilize the end of the sales cycle to get establish new relationships within the customer's business. Why at the end of the sales cycle? Because it is the most likely time for the customer to share information with you, because you are not currently engaged in a sales cycle!

Example: At the close of a sale, I ask the sales professionals who work for me to create a "kick-off event". It is natural for sales professionals to celebrate the sale's close, but the hard account work is just beginning. Successful implementation will require considerable amounts of time, effort and resources from the buyer and the seller. A kick-off event both thanks the customer for their business and ensures implementation gets off to a good start. We typically invite all the key decision makers to the event. The odds of them showing up are surprisingly good. They bought your product and want to know more. They rightly believe that there will be no selling at this meeting. While we are not here to sell, the setting provides an ideal time to ask questions of the decision makers and gather some valuable insights. A kick-off event provide a great environment for several reasons:

- The Sale (at least the original one) is done and there is no pressure on their company to buy anything now.
- The questions you ask are focused on the company's business and future plans.

- People like talking about their own company, and if you ask thoughtful questions, you are likely to get insightful answers.

Said another way: Relax and learn!

If you can demonstrate an ability to help the customer solve other business issues beyond those involved in the current sale, you have taken the first step to embedding not only your product, but also your expertise into the account.

Only a very small percentage of sales professionals choose to focus on the big picture, largely because it is hard work and takes a consulting mind-set.

Sales Thought: Ensure a smooth transition from buyer to customer by establishing the basis of a long-term dialogue with the customer that can help ensure you are around for the next buying cycle.

Sales Tactic: Establish yourself as a Trusted Business Advisor in the first selling process and demonstrate to your new account a commitment after the sale.

13 – Changing the Sale – By connecting business provocation to your value proposition – successful sales people achieve this crucial linkage!

Congratulations, you have identified a potential customer is in the market looking for a product that looks and behaves just like yours. The real question you should ask yourself, and the most overlooked question by most sales people is "understanding": "Why the customer is looking for the product in the first place?"

When faced with a potential sales situation, try "connecting" with the customer with these two steps:

1. Discover the "business provocation" – the business Issue the customer wants your product to address.
2. Once you determine the reason the customer is buying a product, then develop your value proposition to address these defined customer needs.

Developing a value proposition is always an interesting process. First, it is all about your ability to ask good questions so you understand the depth of the customer's need. Second, you have to listen carefully for the real product fit. Usually this Q&A process is all about asking the questions around importance and urgency. Nearly everything that is bought has these 2 characteristics. The sales professional must find the artful combination of importance and urgency that can serve as a value proposition and activate buyer behavior. The key is that it needs to be the right combination of importance and urgency as delivered to the right person!

Sales Thought: Sales professionals know the key to ensuring success is discovering the business provocation and crafting the value proposition that matches the customer's needs.

Avoid throwing all of your product features at the customer at one time and hoping that one of them sticks. It's a major mistake to assume that a particular product will win-out based on nothing more than you reciting features and functions. Without a clear understanding of the customer's true provocation for buying, you run the risk of doing nothing more than confusing the customer with features and functions.

Sales Thought: The customer needs solutions to their problem. Features and functions do not sound like solutions to a customer, but instead sound like sales razzle-dazzle.

Sales professional… go a step beyond. Focus on understanding the customer's business provocation. Until you understand what is "provoking" the customer to be in the market, you are not ready to talk about your product features or functions!

14 – Your sales pitch, no matter how good, will only work for 2% of the customers on the first call.

With these low odds for success on the first call, don't waste time pitching features and functionality. Better to spend your time learning the customer's provocation for buying in your early sales calls. This approach is often referred to as a "discovery call", because the goal of early calls should be to discover the reasons behind the client's need -- the business provocation.

Unless you are selling something so new as to be viewed by your potential customer as a truly "Better Mousetrap," the reality is that you are working with a customer who has probably looked at this issue before, and previously decided the that the timing was not right to address this problem. If the timing is now right for the customer, use the early calls with the Customer to learn the basics.

Sales Tactic: Determine the following:

- Why now?

The problem existed for some time, why is the Customer addressing it now? What has changed?

- Who is it important to? Who is it urgent to?

Understanding this intersection of importance and urgency can paint a better selling picture for us.

Sales Thought: Ask yourself (and the customer!), "Why do they need a product at this particular time?"

Answering this question is the goal of the Discovery Process

Remember, fully 80% of sales are made on the fifth to twelfth contact, so selling is a marathon, not a sprint. It is the rare sales call that will close with a single contact. Given the 2% likelihood for closing the deal in one call, why not take the time to gather the information you need to prepare for your future calls on this client. Gather information by seeking to understand the business provocation. In fact, that should probably be your goal for nearly all first calls on prospective customers.

Sales Thought: Establishing yourself as interested in understanding the client's need – business provocation – will more likely ensure you get to a second call on the potential customer.

15 – Customer collaboration: Do you really get it or just talk the talk?

Let's talk frankly about how the world really operates for sales people in the current sales climate. No matter what you are selling, no one buys from you to "help you out." They won't buy from you because you are a nice person, well dressed, or can articulate a super presentation, show-up with a killer slide deck, and handout a nice looking brochure.

Sales Thought: On a sales call, you are always there to help the customer – not the other way around.

True sales professionals are focused on making the linkage between the customer's stated needs and the products they hope to sell. This type of behavior is the basis of true customer collaboration.

Customer collaboration is not easy. In point of fact it is really hard to do. Customer collaboration requires that you act in a true partnership fashion with the customer and there are 2 things that get in the way of that collaboration:

- Your approach, and
- The customer's reaction to your approach.

Both amount to the same problem; *your approach*

Sales people who focus on partnerships create customer collaborations. The most important skill in collaboration is not the most obvious of skill sets. Presentation skills or product knowledge are not that important in advancing your relationship to a more collaborative state.

Instead, customer collaboration is all about:

- **Questioning for need:** Sales professionals question the customer about their needs to gain an understanding of what the customer wants to accomplish.
- **Linking customer need to your product's capability:** The customer has a business problem and is looking for the most qualified supplier to address that problem.
- **Collaborative behavior:** Ensuring that you are collaborative by being sincere with the customer and establishing a dialogue about business issues, not just talking about product features.

By focusing on the customer business issues and centering the dialogue on understanding customer need, you establish the all-important linkage between business issues and how well your product can address these issues. This becomes the basis for a collaborative relationship.

Example: A successful sales person I coach began making a point of spending more time with customers *after* the Sales Cycle had been closed than anyone else in his particular group. His stated reason was that "I want them to be successful with my product." He found that his customer respected him a *lot* more because of the extra time that he, the Sales Rep, spent on things that were not purely "sales" oriented. As a result, he became much closer to his customer.

The customer began to bring ideas to him, and by being available and interested in their business, he started to make the move towards Trusted Business Advisor. Within a 6-month period, roughly 3 times as fast as any of his fellow sales team I was coaching, he had gained the respect of a large client and was rapidly assisting the client with new, lucrative projects.

16 – Sales move at the speed of TRUST!

So what does trust have to do with the selling process?

Business trust is based on four key principles that you must demonstrate to the customer to proceed with the sale:

1. The customer must believe you fully **understand** their needs.
2. The customer must believe you have the products and skills to **address** their needs.
3. The customer must **believe** you actually will deliver what you promise.
4. The customer must believe you have **their needs** and best interests in mind at all times.

Establishing trust is not an event; it's a process. Loss of trust is an event: it is failure to deliver on any one of the four principles above. In short, trust in a selling situation takes a long time to establish, but only a single event to destroy.

Sales Thought: Your reputation as a selling professional worthy of trust is **the most** valuable asset you have in your tool kit.

What this means in the most basic of terms is that you have chances from the start of the sales process to win your Customer's trust. Depending on what you are selling, this can be a very short process, or it may take some time. In any event, look at each opportunity you have as a unique chance to enhance your professionalism.

So why would you **not** want to establish trust?

Failure to establish trust puts you in a large group, familiar to most buyers – one of the many sellers who come into an account, pitching product.

Where do you want your relationship to evolve to?

By focusing on selling to the Customer the way you would want to be sold to, you put yourself in a different category of seller – that small set of Sellers who don't talk about their Product unless there is a justified business reason presented by the customer for which the Sellers product actually solves the problem.

On indicator that trust is taking place is when you observe the customer presenting new business issues for you to help address. As the customer regularly engages you more deeply in their pressing business issues, asking for advice and counsel on how to best address these issues, you are clearly becoming a Trusted Business Advisor to your customer.

Sales Tactic: Becoming a Trusted Business Advisor is about consistently delivering on the four principles above.

Only Principle 3 has room for maneuvering.

Occasionally, despite your best intentions, deliverables may not be up to agreed to standards, delivery dates, or specifications. As long as the customer perceives you gave it your best effort and you operated within principles 1, 2 and 4, you can recover.

17 – Try a little Zen-like non-selling!

One of most important things to understand if you carry "sales" in your title is that you are one of many! There are a lot of people who carry a sales title; and truthfully, some carry it better than others. So, as a sales person, you have to understand the role you play. You might not think about it as a role, but you do play a critical part.

Sales Thought: Your role is to bring value *to* the products you sell.

Now that might not sound all that complicated. Many sales people mistakenly believe the value of the product or service they sell is self-evident.

You are one of many who do this type of job. So here is some advice that may seem a little strange, but will definitely set you apart from others carrying a sales title:

Sales Thought: Try *not* selling!

Instead of selling, think about how you can help the person you are talking with – your customer – solve a real business issue. If you can do this, you will take an important first step towards bringing value, because you recognize who is helping who. You are helping the customer, not the other way around! You must show how your products and services help the customer if the customer is to help you by placing an order.

Simply looking at your products and services may not fire up the customer enough to place an order. Your brochure and slide deck, while good, probably won't do this either. It is you that brings the magic to the show.

Sellers that focus on the big picture have the greatest chance to be viewed in a different light. By focusing on learning (from and about the customer) and not selling, the Seller can demonstrate to the Customer knowledge of the business issues that are top of mind to the Customer. By Taking this approach, a different kind of relationship can emerge – one where the Customer will call on the Seller to act as that rarest of all Seller- the Trusted Business Advisor.

How Buyer/Seller relationship evolves is rarely either ideal or perfect. It involves the Seller asking questions on the fly – taking the information they hear and using the information to craft execution possibilities for the Customer.

So try not selling anything on your next sales call. That doesn't mean being indifferent to helping the customer, but instead be genuinely unconcerned about making the sale during this sales call. Spend the time talking with the customer, understanding their business needs, and establishing your credentials as a sales professional.

18 – Another round of Zen selling principles....

Sales Thought: Non-selling doesn't mean not getting the sale. It means earning the sale.

In order to bring value to the customer, focus on what the customer is trying to accomplish, **not** what you are trying to accomplish. Instead of selling, help the customer achieve their ends. If you can find a way to **legitimately** connect what the customer is trying to accomplish to what you sell – and here I mean without a stretch, passing the red face test – then you have a chance to bring real value to the customer. If on the other hand, you cannot legitimately help solve the customer's problem with your product, then help them solve it with another viable solution.

The way successful sales people create Zen-like selling is through a well thought out series of questions that help lead to a fundamental **insight** for the seller and, perhaps more importantly, for the customer. This insight and understanding about what the customer really wants to accomplish may be beyond what the customer initially understood.

And, if you are really sharp, this insight experienced by the customer brings value – and a sale.

When customers achieve an insight through interacting with you, they more fully understand the value you bring to them is value beyond the product and sale.

Selling Tactic: Try not Selling and don't get defensive if you are questioned about why you are asking so many questions!

Sales Thought: Be Zen-like! If you don't sell, then you have a better chance of being viewed as a Trusted Business Advisor!

TWO – ACCOUNT PLANNING

First Thoughts

Some of you may skip past this section entirely because you don't presently do Account Planning. In spite of this, I would encourage you to reconsider, as this section will help you do a better job of setting up expectations with your customers and taking them down a preferred pathway.

For those of you that don't want to be engaged in Account Planning, here is one thought: If you are not doing this with your key customers, what are the odds that one of your competitors IS? This may help you understand why you should be doing Account Planning - Where you are an individual Seller or you work with a Team.

In both situations the notion of Account Planning will bring value. It is especially important when you have to coordinate Team Oriented activities.

1 – Definition of Account Planning: A dynamic, Ever Changing Plan that ensures greater and long term Sales success.

Planning is something that most sales professionals say they want to do. That is until they realize that Account Planning requires actually having to update/upgrade the way they interact with Customers. This proves to be a sticking point with some sales professionals, but those that choose to go down this account planning path, often separate themselves from the vast majority of Sellers.

The key element is to always be sure to understand your customer's Ever-evolving needs. This means that you need to stay current on your customer's business status. If you don't do this, the odds are that whatever you position (plan to sell) will be out of date with customer needs. Account Planning is labeled "dynamic" for a good reason: Proper Plans are updated in an ongoing basis based on ever changing work with the particular Customer.

To be effective, the Account Planning Process must include several Elements:

- **Dynamic:** The plan is continually changing, because things are continually changing. The Planning Process is ever changing, because that is the nature of most successful relationships with Clients
- **Team-oriented:** Getting the right Resources from the Customer Engaged with the Seller or Selling Team, ensuring that all who will interact with the Customer will form a unified front in their interaction with the Customer
- **Relationship-based:** Unless you are selling today's version of a "Hot" Product, building and maintaining a Relationship with your Buyer will make or break 95% of all Selling situations.
- **Collaborative:** Working both with your organization and then with the Customer Elevates how the Customer will think about the Seller and/or Selling organization.

- **Ever evolving:** In this day and age Plans have to be updated on an ever-increasing basis. Tis this the sign of a bad plan? Quite the Contrary, in most cases, it is the sign of a very good plan. As Progress is made, the plan needs to be updated to reflect the progress that has been made and where we will next work on advancing the work we are doing with each Customer.

Example: I recently coached a sales team that was working with a potentially large Customer that had previously not done business with my client. I coached the sales team to focus on creating a plan that had 4 elements and presenting the plan, along with asking questions about the plan's fit for the customer. The team engaged the customer in the plan and thinking about the overall account. The Customer was struck by the change. As a direct result of this changed approach, the Sales Team closed a significant sale. When the Vice President who had signed the contract was asked: "Why did you chose this Vendor?", he replied, "They stopped just Selling to us and began to really work with us to address a series of our most pressing business issues."

2 – There are 3 Elements of Success for *any* account.

In my work with sales teams, I have seen teams go from where they had:

- No Relationships with anyone at the buyers business they were trying to sell to
- No Pipeline for sales
- No successful users of their product

… to an evolution where they were able to get the Customer not only using their product but also buying more of it to address other Business issues at that particular customer. This is most often achieved by ensuring that you are doing all three things at once:

- **Relationship** – is not parachuting people in to have dinner with a Prospect, it is about building a real relationship
- **Pipeline** – is not about selling one deal – it is about outlining to the Customer how your product can help them not only address their current business Issue, but other issues in the long run.
- **Customer Success** – Focusing on making sure that once they are sold, that the Company you work for will help them be successful with the product.

Relationship: In the era of social networking, *real* relationships are more important than ever. Buyers want to know that there vendors really care – and not just when there is a deal on the table. Tools such as LinkedIn are just that – tools. You will flounder in the long run unless you are investing in real relationships.

Pipeline: Thinking beyond the deal at hand is essential. Unless you are selling a once in a lifetime product, a smart seller will focus on not just selling now, but making the people you are selling to customers for the long run. This is not about trying to sell more right now. The focus it is on the big picture and helping the customer understand where you can help them next. Sellers who do this invariably have more success, as they create a ready pipeline as they sell.

Customer Success: The nature of Selling for the sales professional is not about selling and moving on to the next Prospect. But rather it is about ensuring that each Customer sold is successful using the product they just purchased.

Example: One of the most common things I hear people saying, is "I don't get paid to make **them** successful. That is someone else's job." There is no way sellers who believe this statement can be can be very successful in the long run, mainly because they are giving up 3 distinct sales opportunities that determine long-term sales success:

- Repeat business – selling more at the same company
- Word of mouth business – referrals from satisfied customers
- Tag-along business – following customers to their next company

These 3 types of business are essential sources of long-term sales success. Focusing on Relationship, Pipeline, and Customer Success will increase your chances of having long-term sales success and picking up the easy wins, versus having to start cold with every sales call.

Sales Thought: You may land some big deals, but Buyers remember when they are not treated well. They remember the Seller who sold them and then "Vanished like a Thief in the Night." It is an old joke, but is closer to the truth than you might think.

3 – Great Sales Teams focus on the end game and don't get caught up in "activity for activity's sake." (Especially near year's end!)

It is very typical for a Sales Team to have a major focus on "year end." The problem is: If one is narrowly focused on the current sale, it can cause a lot of problems.

One of the most frequent symptoms of "short-term behavior" is when you get caught up in activity that may or may not be sending you down a good path. This is also called "activity for activity's sake." The problem is that, in most businesses, while year's end is important, it can cause you to veer away from more effective sales behavior, such as:

- Understanding your customer's evolving needs.
- Staying current on your customer's business status.

It's great for a Sales Team to set targets and goals. It is not so great to show the customer that all you care about is the "next deal." Here is a decision that everyone in sales has to make:

Choice 1: All that matters is the next deal, OR

Choice 2: You focus on the long run; bringing value to each customer you work with.

It's a clear decision for you to make.

Taking Choice 1 means that you will get some short-term deals. It may also mean that you lose sight of the big picture and overall focus on the customer's most urgent needs. Sometimes a sales professional feels pressured to make this choice, especially when management treats sales objectives like a moving goal post in football.

Choice 2 may mean you sacrifice some short-term revenue, but you form a better and more long-lasting relationship with your customer. It is a decision that most people in sales have to make from time to time. There is no "right and wrong" in this situation. It depends on what you sell, who you sell to, and how you want to be positioned for the long run.

Sales Thought: No matter which one you choose, don't get caught up in "activity for activity's sake."

Example: One Sales Team I know struggled with a mandate they had from management to make a "specific number of calls" on certain accounts that were considered to be important to the business. Instead of simply going down that path of increasing call volume, the Sales Team approached management with a plan to set up a different type of call quality and purpose. Rather than hammering away with a fixed set of questions, a quality dialogue was established that produced strategic outcomes for the Sales Team and the customers. The customers appreciated this new contact approach. The new customer dialogue focused on helping the Sales Team learn about new and emerging opportunities and avoided a narrow focus on how things were going with the existing project.

Sales Thought: It is possible to expand activity with your existing clients if you are focused on a true end game defined by customer collaboration, not just the next deal.

4 – Do not confuse selling with developing a Strategic Account Plan. Just because you can sell doesn't mean you are automatically strategic.

Many successful sales people get the job done because they are good at "getting deals done." Nothing wrong with this and, at some companies, it is the clear way to be successful. However, something interesting happens when you go from being a sales person to being a "strategic" seller. For some customers and, for some sales people, it is all about deals. However, sometimes that's not enough!

Remember, the old: "price drop" technique has gone the way of the dinosaur.

If you are currently in sales and suddenly you are transferred to the role of being a strategic sales person with key customer accounts, things have to change!

Strategic sellers have to look at things a little differently than they did before taking on this role. Now you have to learn about things like this:

- How does your customer do business? What are the businesses needs going forward?
- How do your products help the customer achieve their goals?
- Do you have a plan in order to achieve your goal in working with that particular customer?

To go from sales person to strategic seller requires that you have a plan to get there. You can't just say you are going to be a strategic seller.

For certain sales people, it is important to understand the role you are in and where you want to go!

If it's important to act as a strategic provider, you have to invest to get there. For sellers, this is a fundamental change in the way to go about doing business!

Sales Thought: Developing a Strategic Account Plan is a different skill base than simply being in sales. You can do it, but a lot of learning is required to make the transition. Are you up for it, or do you just want to "get deals done?"

Example: I was asked to consult with several sales people from the same group, all of whom had been successful. They were then asked to put together their plans on a going forward basis. Initially, they thought they could do it by themselves but, upon review, management made this comment on every plan:

"This isn't a plan. It's just how to get the next deal done! Where is the plan going forward?"

I worked with each team and focused them on the bigger picture, getting them to think about the long-term plan. It was a different set of questions than they had been asked before, and different items had to be done to fulfill the plan. They ended up with a very good strategic plan, and each team was successful in their next year of execution by focusing on the longer-term!

5 – A Sales Process works only if EVERYONE from top to bottom of the organization is committed to using it.

Most businesses have trouble addressing the need for an Account Planning Process that is truly used throughout the organization. Actually, if it is just for the Sales Team, it can't be called a true process. A Sales Process requires buy-in from all of those that can impact it. If not, then the Sales Team might work through their issues only to have their process overridden by other people in the organization.

This problem becomes particularly acute for Strategic Accounts. If a Sales Team is following a process specifically designed to help the company better act in a strategic fashion, and if others override the process, it will surely fail, as will the relationship with that particular client.

Sales Thought: If the entire selling company is NOT using the process, it is probably not strategic.

There are many ways to overcome this issue. Here are some sample approaches:

- Establish ONE Sales Process that applies to all of your customers. You may have to make some exceptions for more strategic or significant accounts, but at least you will start off with a single process you can work from.
- Ensure that THE process is indeed just that, THE process and everyone in the organization, from top to bottom, follows it.
- As your organization grows, update the process to reflect the sophistication and complexity that comes with growth.
- Don't continuously re-invent the sales process or ignore it. Execution based on a consistently utilized process, one that everyone follows, will almost always be superior to just "winging it".

Execute to the best of your abilities, but don't change the process for just one client or one big deal. Find a way to execute and remind everyone that it is about executing from top to bottom if you are to be successful!

Example: I was consulting with a company where the CEO completely removed himself from the selling process and turned it over to other members of the Corporate Leadership Team. We told the CEO and his Direct Reports that, if they did engage in a Process that went from the Top to Bottom of the organization, they would see meaningful improvement in their Results. While the CEO was somewhat shocked with this, they decided to move forward with the strategy we recommended.

With the Implementation of a Company Wide Process that held all accountable for various parts of the Customer Engagement Process, Sales increased by 15% year over year and the Sales Teams felt truly connected to rest of the organization for the first time.

Sales Thought: The Sales Team must feel connected to the entire organization if they are to act as effective agents to the marketplace.

6 – How to be a Strategic seller and Sales Team while working in a non-strategic company.

There are many times when I meet with sales professionals who want to be more strategic in their selling, but they are working for a company that does not sell strategically. What they do instead is keep pushing for immediate revenue.

Some Sales Professionals can work well in a pure transactional environment – an environment with short-term selling approach. There are other sales professionals who *think* strategically, but struggle to try to *act* strategically while working in an environment that does not reward strategic selling.

There *is* a strategy that does get the best out of strategic sellers working in a non-strategic selling environment.

Sales Professionals can build an account plan that reflects a flow from the immediate business issues facing the buyer, to setting vision with the buyer.

Sales Tactic: Move from addressing an issue that is front and center to the Buyer that can be immediately addressed with a sale, to working toward a longer-term vision for the account.

Vision Sellers are often accused of not thinking in the best interest of the company that employs them, as they might be seen to not be taking quick orders. "We need Revenue *now*, you can't spend time trying to Set Vision!" is the way that a frustrated manager might speak to a vision-based Seller.

The comeback from the Seller is key. A shrewd strategic Seller must satisfy their manager's short-term demands *and* address the Buyer's longer-term needs.

Example: Coaching a Seller caught between her need to sell strategically and her company's short-term selling focus, I helped her see that the Buyer had an immediate need for certain of her products. We first focused on these products with the Buyer.

What she did was:

- Find and satisfy an immediate need of the Buyer, and therefore her manager.
- Confirm that the Buyer saw how the Immediate Business Issue could be solved
- Then she demonstrated product capabilities that were not needed now, but future capabilities the Buyer saw could address future business needs.

These steps had the dual effect of ensuring that while the current business Issues were addressed for the Buyer and for her manager, there was a vision set with the Buyer for the future – a vision that the Seller could come back to with the buyer when the time was right.

This approach allowed the strategic Seller to live in both worlds and satisfy both the Buyer and her manager.

The setting of a vision with the Buyer while solving and immediate needs speaks directly to the notion on how the seller's solutions can serve the Buyer – both now and in the future.

Sellers with short-term selling processes that want to sell strategically should try these techniques for key accounts, particularly accounts where there is great long-term potential for growth, but where that long-term relationship with the Buyer would be lost by focusing only on a quick sale.

7 – Selling Processes are NOT the enemy. Poor execution of Sales Process *is the* problem that usually screams out for attention in many organizations.

This is usually an issue of selling Companies not getting it. Many times, they are just moving so fast that they don't really know how to bring it all together and Implement a Process that both Drives Revenue and ensures proper execution.

In 2014 many people think that selling is all about "art," "gut feel", and "winging" it. While many view it as a classic battle of art versus science, I think there are solid elements of both. Good Sales Processes demand a logical merger of both.

There are some business leaders who don't believe in Sales Process at all.

Unfortunately, some business leaders think that sales people just "do it." While this sales-as-an-art-form approach may be true in some organizations, it is not the case in the majority – and certainly not the norm for the big players. Look around. Major sales organizations have invested in sophisticated Sales Processes that empower and support their sales people.

The leaders know that a well-implemented Sales Process, backed by the organization at all levels, ensures that Sales Professionals can effectively sell *and* deliver value to each customer!

When an organization begins to grow, a decently designed Sales Process will help sustain growth. Without a *real* process, any organization can and will run into issues around execution in one or more areas.

Warning signs that you need a Sales Process (or signs your current process is no longer adequate):

1. Approvals become harder to get.
2. More rules start to interfere with the process

3.   Senior management gets personally involved in deals.
4.   People feel they are hampered from getting their job done.
5.   People feel that it's harder to work inside the organization than outside.
6.   The Sales Team is constantly apologizing to customers or making excuses about the Sales Process.

These are the signs of an organization that has not properly implemented an effective Sales Process!

The solution is pretty straightforward: Implement a Sales Process that helps Sales Professionals turn opportunity and inquiry from the customer into delivery of solutions.

Effective Sales Process is not a bad thing or something to be avoided. Instead, Sales Process is about insuring execution from beginning to end!

The best sales professionals understand how to use an effective Sales Process and work within it. Complaining about using an effective Sales Process is like complaining about being healthy.

Sales Thought: While an effective Sales Process is likely to require more work, lack of a formal Sales Process will certainly mean important sales and business will be missed!

8 – Make sure you keep your sales process relevant to the marketplace and workable for the sales team.

Sales professional who chafe at following a process may or may not have a point.

I have observed situations where the sales planning process for a start-up company began as an effective sales approach. As the company grew, the leadership saw no need to change the sales approach. When sales begin to languish, sales leadership, and most particularly the founders, thought that the answer was for the sales team to work harder.

If your business started out in a garage, with five people, fine, but the sales process for a start-up has a lifespan based on company growth. As an organization grows, it has to have new sales eyes come in with a fresh look at how the sales process is working; or not working.

As the organization finally came to grips with their sales process problem, it was determined that new planning steps – and in some cases new people – would be injected into a reformulated selling approach. The new sales process included new rewards systems that ensured that those that were doing a good job would be rewarded and streamlined processes – reducing process steps from weeks down to days, or in some cases hours.

Sales Thought: Always address the sales process situation *as it is now* – not how it was in the past – or how it might be in the future.

Smart company's continuously evaluate the relevance of their sales process for the marketplace and assess the workability for the sales team. Growing companies make continuous adjustments to their sales process based on the marketplace that exists *today*!

9 – Focus on acting as a Sales Team: Bring ALL your available resources to bear on key accounts!

Working as a team is critical to success. Team selling has become more important as customers have become better informed. Customers can more fully keep up with what is going on by utilizing the Internet and other readily available resources. This way they generally know all about your business, your products, and your reputation in the marketplace. They also have deep questions about your products and business practices.

Most sales people cannot provide the level and array of information demanded by this new breed of well-informed customers. While Sales Professionals can attempt to provide all the answers, we must seriously consider the time-cost to the sales person and what impacts will encroach on the Customer Relationship.

There was a time when some sales people were successful by keeping everyone out of their accounts. This technique was called "Commando Selling." While you *can* do this today, there are better techniques that will help you achieve more consistent success.

Today, your customers expect to receive high levels of service and product information that can help them become more successful. Focus on being a source of information and resources to your customer. I call this "marshaling resources." As a master of marshaling resources you accomplish two very important things:

1. The marshaling resources strategy represents a level of organizational maturity and sales-ability that many organizations cannot deliver.
2. You have the chance to separate yourself into an elite level of sales person by demonstrating this level of attention to detail to your Buyer.

Finally, remember this:

If you don't take this approach, what makes you think your competition won't outsell and out-execute you?

For your most important accounts – perhaps called "Strategic Accounts" in your company – you need to bring a **team** of people to work together to be successful.

Example: I was asked to work with a sales person who was considered very good, but a bit of a loner within his organization. His account team was frustrated because they felt there was a lot more they could do but they were not allowed to participate as much as was needed for such a critical Strategic Account. He made all the decisions. After some time together, we reformulated the account plan and involved the account team in more of the activities. This resulted in a much happier working environment and the closing of the largest deal in the company's history. Teaming does work and often results in a great environment for the entire Sales Team.

10 – Account Planning is a process, not an event. The next sale is just one step in the process.

Many sales people I have worked with over the years think of planning as a "checking the box" exercise. Too many sales people focus on the next deal and how they can get that "next big one" positioned for landing. This clearly works for a small segment of sales people. Ask yourself this: If you are working with a large account, do you want the customer to think of you as being a strategic partner or a sales person? If being a strategic partner is your goal, then set about establishing a plan that benefits everyone involved:

- The sales person
- The Sales Team
- The company
- And, most particularly, the Customer

For most of your accounts, it is helpful to maintain a rolling 3-month planning horizon for each account. It's a good idea not to just work a "task list," but to focus on the bigger picture:

- What are your annual and quarterly goals and objectives for each customer?
- Are you going to meet them?
- Are you aligned with customer expectations?

Think about what you want to accomplish beyond just the next deal. If the next deal is your whole planning horizon and focus, then there's a problem. You probably aren't aware that you could work with this customer on a strategic – big picture-long-term basis. Further, your customer will soon recognize that selling is your only focus.

It's important to have a clear understanding of your customer if you plan to create a long-term future. This requires that you spend some time understanding the customer and focusing on how both you and the customer can benefit from a long-term planning process. Strategic relationships require you to become well versed in what the customers want to accomplish for their business and how you can help them get there.

If you are not willing or able to invest the time in creating a plan based on a long-term planning horizon for the customer, PLUS work the plan you create, you have reduced the probability of having a successful long-term customer relationship.

Example*:* I recently coached a sales professional who was selling to a large telecom company. My client did a very good job of getting the relationship started with a product sale. It turned out the product she sold was a perfect fit for the identified business problem. But when the customer began making additional support demands, her organization balked at providing additional support and resources to the account. Her up-line leadership was not interested in a long-term sales process, nor were they interested in the strategic sales objectives and support outlined in the plan she had developed with the customer. Instead, her up-line leadership chose to focus on short-term revenue results.

Her inability to work her written long-term sales plan opened the door to a competitor who was willing to invest time, money and effort to demonstrate that they understood the telecom company's needs for support were part of a longer term relationship

While her competitor could not undo her first sale, they were able to demonstrate to the telecom that they understood the value of the business and would be willing to invest in a long-term business relationship.

Sales Tactic: Demonstrating to the customer that you understand what they need for success and are willing to "invest" in the account is the key to developing and sustaining long-term sales success.

Revenues with large clients, like a telecom company, are part of the overall account planning process, not a one-time sale. Her competitor knew this and used a long-term approach to get in the door. This paved the way for her competitor to develop a long-term relationship with the telecom customer. Her company got a single sale, but no additional business.

Sales Thought: If you are not willing to invest in an account plan to establish a long-term customer relationship, don't plan on having sustained success in the account, particularly with large, sophisticated companies.

If you are not willing or able to plan further out than one quarter for a customer relationship, then you don't really have a relationship.

11 – Managers and Sales Execs: If you don't believe in Strategic Sales Planning, don't make your sales profession do it!

What you sell and the complexity of your product should drive your selling methodology. There are schools of thought that focus on simply focusing on "getting the next deal." There is nothing wrong with this approach, particularly if your focus is just transaction-to-transaction. And it's okay if that is how you want to run your sales organization. But, if getting the next deal is how you want to drive your Sales Team, you have to accept the fact that you will likely be viewed as a transaction seller. If transaction selling is where you want to be, I am not here to tell you it's wrong. The reality is transaction-to-transaction selling can be a successful approach. The downside is that your customers will never view you as a strategic vendor.

If you want to establish deeper relationships with an account, you have to develop a plan to drive the account relationship forward.

Some sales managers and sales executives just want to have their cake and eat it too. They want to be both a strategic vendor with key customer accounts - developing long-term relationships within the account - AND want the sales professionals who work for them to get deals done in a hurry. Rarely do the two approaches mix well in practice.

Expecting deeper account penetration AND quick sales is often unrealistic. You have to make the time (take the time) to act deliberately with certain key customers. When you do take the time to plan the account and execute the plan, you make a decision to act in a more strategic fashion.

Developing Strategic Sales Plans for key customers is not enough. Some sales managers and executives think that simply developing a strategic plan for key clients will change how the Sales Team operates. Rarely does this happen! Once your Sales Teams have developed plans, sales managers and executives have to ensure it is executed as planned, regularly re-evaluated, and that the Sales Team is continuing to follow the plan.

Many sales leaders take the time to build plans for key customers, but few effectively manage the strategic plans their Sales Teams create. In this case, the sales manager or sales executive doesn't really believe in Strategic Account Planning. They seem to think that, if they build partial plans, everything will change. It won't. If you don't believe in Strategic Sales Planning processes, don't try to fake it.

Example: A classic case I recently observed involved senior management mandating account planning for all key accounts – the 10% of accounts responsible for major revenue. The sales team, from manager on down, had followed the process and built a strong account plan. The manager, however, was merely complying with directives and not interested in actually implementing the plan.

When it came time to take the plan to the customer (a part of the mandated account planning process), the sales team panicked. They realized that, while they had built a good plan, they had not actually taken any steps toward implementing it.

The customer figured it out pretty quickly. The lack of plan implementation indicated to the customer that the account team was clearly out of touch and didn't value their business. The customer began to seek new options and the account, not surprisingly, was soon lost.

Sales Tactic: Build the account plan, and then work with the customer to execute the plan on a consistent basis.

Sales Thought: If you as, a sales manager or sales director, don't believe in planning, just say no to building strategic account plans. Without commitment from above, and a willingness of the team to implement, planning is generally a great waste of everyone's time.

Sadly, it' might be better for some selling organizations to simply send the Sales Team out "to just get the deals" than to pretend the strategic account plans are valuable.

12 – Senior Management: If your Sales Teams create Strategic Account Plans, YOU must actively manage results against those plans.

Strategic Account Planning is a time consuming activity for a Sales Team. The most important thing is that the plans be actively utilized. If not actively utilized by the sales organization or selling company, particularly senior sales management, they will rapidly become nothing but make-work.

Sales management needs to show that it doesn't just give lip service to planning. A Strategic Account Plan must be in place and used by everyone from the sales person to the senior sales manager involved. If not, the Sales Team will rapidly realize that Strategic Account Plans are a waste of time.

Sales Thought: A good strategy is for senior sales executives to ensure that, once built, Strategic Account plans are being reviewed and tracked by senior management.

The most important thing is that the plan remains a living document that will continue to be used and updated along with progress with the particular account.

Periodically, the plan needs to be "refreshed" based on current activity at the account. When it is refreshed, this is also a good time to review it with Senior Management. This step ensures continued oversight and buy-in at all levels within the selling organization.

Strategic Account Planning cannot start with and stop with the Sales Team creating the plans. Strategic Account Planning must be used by the entire management team to ensure it will be supported by the entire selling organization, from top to bottom.

Strategic Account Plans, properly implemented and reviewed, are *the* critical tool for senior management to drive sales to strategic customers. They ensure that strategically identified customers are targeted through planning and that the sales organization is implementing a plan for acquiring and retaining valuable customers.

While investing the time and resources necessary for a Strategic Account plan may not be appropriate for all customers, for those customers that really matter they are essential.

Example: One of my favorite client stories is of a small software company and how they strategically addressed the needs of a really large manufacturing company. The manufacturing company was a customer, but not yet a big customer. However, the small software company saw the account potential and really believed that the manufacturer could be a much larger customer IF they were given some special care.

So, a very strong Strategic Account Plan was put in place. The Plan was implemented and upgraded on a consistent basis. The manufacturing company was kept updated and involved in formal account plan reviews. The manufacturer observed that the small software company was investing in the account and really providing the attention they expected. The account has grown and the strategic relationship between the manufacturer and the software company continues to grow.

Sales Thought: If your sales organization is investing time and resources in creating Strategic Account Plans, then smart sales managers and executives should capitalize on that investment by fully utilizing the plans.

13 – Planning is NOT a dirty word to true Sales Professionals.

Planning is a key ingredient in making true Sales Professionals excellent within the craft. Planning makes good sales professionals great. Planning ensures effective execution with key sales accounts and enables consistent performance across accounts. Planning focuses the entire Sales Team by setting an end goal for each account and defines roles and responsibilities for each selling situation.

Good plans include key items that need to be done and a timeframe for completion. Some items are short-term, but many planned selling steps require long-term focus. The key is to create plans you can follow throughout ever-changing sales cycles. Things will keep changing at the company you are working with. It's important to have a plan in place, modify the plan as changing circumstances dictate, and continue to follow the plan. Keep the plan up to date.

Sales Thought: Having a written plan for each key account is a defining difference between successful Sales Professionals and all others.

Planning enables sales professionals to control the game, set the sales table, and be proactive (not reactive) to customers. Solid planning in advance gives you the ability to work in a proactive fashion, a skill customers will recognize as a differentiator. Planning helps prevent reactive "fire drills" at your accounts that cause your customers to worry about your ability to execute after the sale. True sales professionals always focus on being proactive and a solid account plan is key.

Planning is focused on ensuring that the entire Sales Team is working from the same overall plan. It doesn't mean that you do the same thing, all the time, the same way for each customer. But it does mean that you have an overall "Game Plan" for how you will work with the rest of your selling teammates. Not having a written plan means there is no plan and no leadership on the account. This means you and the rest of the team will be reacting to your customer's wishes. If reacting doesn't sound like a good place to be, focus on developing a plan!

Example: One compelling example involved a company with a broad range of products for manufacturing companies. For one of their particularly important manufacturing accounts, they had a variety of resources working on different parts of the account and not coordination among the account team. As your might expect, with no plan there was constant conflict between the various members of the sales team.

Lack of a Strategic Account Plan (and this was a hugely strategic account!) lead to selling confusion and a frustrated customer. There was a real risk of losing the account. Finally, the Sales Team collaborated on an overall account plan. Putting the plan together took an investment of time, but paid dividends in the form of smoother execution and a much happier customer.

Don't wait until the lack of a plan impacts selling performance and the customer's perception of your company. Key customers require Strategic Account Plans.

Sales Thought: Planning is *not* a dirty word or a waste of time for the sales professional. Planning allows you to be proactive with key customers.

14 –Get your client to buy-in to key parts of the plan.

To really advance the relationship to the "Next Level," in most cases requires that we being to focus on Collaborative Planning with the Customer.   This requires a change in how each side invests in the relationship:

- **For the Seller:** It is about selling more, and in order to sell more, you are prepared to invest money and time in building out the Relationship, and ensuring customer success.

- **For the Buyer (Customer)**: It is about investing time to ensure that the Seller is successful and will continue to want to invest time.

It is a Mutual Relationship that requires on-going re-evaluation of where we are going and where we could go.

Example: A company that sells complex machinery began to establish jointly execution plans with their customers. The machinery manufacturer executed a planned series of steps with the intent to get their Customers to a point where they would make a Commitment to the Purchase. This had the effect of making the Customer part of the process, while ensuring that the customer had skin in the game. While this won't work for every selling situation, as varies depending on what you sell, it is a good technique to get the Customer more bought in to your plan and execution.

The Sales Process should not be a battleground.

Selling is traditionally viewed as an adversarial situation. You are trying to get someone to buy something. Because making a buying decision can be very tense situation, the buyer may feel under a lot of pressure to part with their money. Therefore, in most cases, the buyer might think of you as the agent that is creating an adversarial relationship.

Sales Thought: One of the most important things to try to do in any sales situations is to make the sale, as much as possible, a partnership between you and the buyer. It is critical to establish open lines of communication to an open partnership.

By taking a partnership approach you can minimize, or at least cut down on, any perception of an adversarial relationship the buyer may perceive is being built up. Sellers who use a partnership approach typically have more success in getting to the end of the Sales Cycle in a good place. Sales professionals work to remove the adversarial perceptions of the buyer by establishing a partnership environment. Framing the sales process as a mutual effort – a partnership – can change the thoughts the Buyer has about the Seller.

Sales Thought: Help your client experience partnership in the selling process by outlining a selling approaches to the buyer as a set of steps that will be get the process of buying done in a fashion that **both** the seller and buyer have input.

Removing the buyer's perceptions of an adversarial buying process is not always easy to pull off. It largely involves give and take on both sides of equation, but the key word we should utilize here is *mutual*. If things are being done mutually, then both sides are in it together!

Sales Tactic: Executing a step-by-step plan that helps the client acquire the product you are selling generally yields success.

Sales Thought: One of the things to remember is that the Buy/Sell Relationship is based on a misconception of conflict. If you have a product the customer needs, then there is not conflict.

When it comes down to it for real, you generally sell a **lot** more than your Customer will buy. Depending on the scope of the sale, your buyer might not even know all the steps that have to be done from a buying perspective. By putting a mutually developed plan in place, you can **help** the buyer rapidly get to a point where they you working with them and assisting in the Sales Process.

The other thing to remember here is that your Buyer will not put all their cards on the table if you don't show that you are there to help. Through a set of questions and answers that are asked early in the process, it comes down to ensuring there is Mutual Trust and Respect throughout the Buying Process.

Sales Thought: You sell every day, but most clients buy seldom. They are relative novices in the process and therefore tend to be inefficient at getting their needs met.

Selling should not be a battleground. Help your client through a structure buying process to get to yes faster.

15 – If you can work together as a Sales Team, you often control the sale and account game by establishing the rules, and not playing someone else's game!

Today one of the most important aspects of selling is knowing how to appropriately utilize a team of people in a sales situation. The traditional view of the sales approach involves a sales professional totally in control of the buying environment. Frankly, most sales professionals not only want to be in control of the sales cycle, but admit to feeling better when they hold all the levers in the deal.

Sales Thought: One of the most important things to consider: In most situations, if you cannot work with your team to establish a set of steps they will help you execute, then it will be very hard for you to work with your customer in any kind of a partnership.

Tackling your personal need to control everything is essential for success. There's nothing wrong with feeling the need for account control but, in a complex sales cycle, a lot of people have to typically be involved in the buying decision.

Sales Thought: Sales Professionals have to evolve from a notion of control to a concept of coordination. In today's very complex Selling environment, control is usually an Illusion. Sellers rarely control things. Good Sellers coordinate many aspects of the Sale with a team, and this is what makes them successful Sellers.

Continue to wrestle with your personal need to control everything. While there is nothing wrong with feeling the need for account control, remember in a complex sales cycle, there are typically a lot of people involved in the buying decision and you need matching expertise from the selling side.

Sales Thought: You cannot be an expert on every technical aspect of the sale and competently answer every question the buyers team will have; the client will know this even if you don't.

16 – For complex sales, you need resources on your side to work with the resources on the prospect's side. Resources are essential to move a prospect to the point of wanting to be a customer.

One of the most important roles that a sales person can take on is that of coordinator of account resources. An effective sales professional is able to bring resources to bear on their accounts. The result is accounts that recognize that their account representative is not just a sales person, but is a trusted resource at the selling company. By taking on the resource coordination role, the sales professional demonstrates to the customer ongoing value after the sale.

Sales Tactic: Don't overlook a key sales resource at your disposal – your senior executive team.

For potentially large and complicated sales, you may need to have multiple senior executives from your company speak with senior executives at the prospect. This step is important to seal the deal with new accounts. It signals commitment and relationship building with the prospect and can greatly increase your likelihood of making a sale.

Sales Thought: When there are a lot of experts and disciplines involved in the buying decision, it's important to have a team on the selling side which can match up to the team of people on the buyer's side.

The notion of Team Based Selling may be new to your organization of the Buyers organization. Your team can help you work with the Buyer's team on this team concept by helping establish the rules for the buy. Your team, working with the Buyer's team, can collectively determine the decision criteria for the buy much easier than you can alone.

Key Steps in setting the buying criteria:

- Get the customer buying team to agree to a set of rules for making the buy decision.
- Jointly set the rules for determining the buy.
- Set rules that you feel are good for you.

If the Customer sees that you are logically working toward a decision that was jointly framed, and providing them with the agreed to information they need to make the decision, you can often then get them to agree to establish a set of rules for the evaluation that is mutually beneficial to both customer and seller.

Once again, nothing is perfect. Sometimes the Customer just feels that they have to be in control of the evaluation from start to finish. In this situation, the Seller has to make up his or her mind about what they are going to do, and how much they will play the evaluation game by rules that do not benefit the Seller.

17 – You cannot be an expert on every technical aspect of the sale. You cannot competently answer every question the buyer's team will have. The client will know this even if you don't.

The notion of team-based selling may be new in your sales environment. Working as a team can assist you in one of the most important aspects of selling – answering the prospect team's detailed questions. Think about how often you can present to a variety of experts on the prospect's side of the table. Each of them has a depth of knowledge in some aspect of your product or service. In fact, each of them is expert in an area that you may have only general knowledge about while each has unique needs.

Sales Tactic: To address all the prospect team's questions in a complex sale, use a team-based selling approach.

In 2014, the amount of information that is available makes the selling job harder because Prospects have much more information available. As such, Sellers have to be prepared to work in the Team environment to ensure that questions are answered. Stated another way, one of the biggest differences in Sales now is fundamental change to a Teaming Approach often makes the difference between those who win and those who lose.

Stated another way, the fundamental change in how sales people *used to be* seen as, to borrow military parlance:

Commandos: Guys who can go in and are in charge of things and go full bore in every situation. Commandos were in control.

I have told sales People the World over as of late that "Control is an Illusion. In this day and age, the most you can hope for is Coordination. With the Vast amount of information that Buyers have in their hands, Sellers need to be Coordinators: Ensuring that information gets to buyers in an organized fashion. Those Sellers that insist that they are *"in control"* will have a very difficult time being successful. They will find that they are behind the sales curve and unable to keep up with the flow information in the Sales Process, circa 2014.

18 – For a straighter path to a buy decision, make sure the Customer buying team agrees on the decision criteria (rules) for the buy.

If you can get the Customer buying team to agree on a set of rules for making the buying decision, your path to the sale becomes clear and objective. Working with the customer to jointly set the rules for determining the buy is a high level sales skill and takes some practice to implement. Think about what you are doing with this approach… you are creating an agenda for working together, with clear expectations outlined from the start. Most importantly, a jointly developed set of rules for making the buying decision removes the guesswork for the sales professional.

Selling (and buying) with the rules jointly created is a rational, logical approach that helps both parties work toward mutually beneficial outcomes, using the same rules.

Sales Thought: Make sure to also set rules that you feel are good for you.

Willingness of an existing customer to jointly set rules is a great test of the status of your existing Customer relationship.

Your alternative to jointly planning the buying rules and criteria with the customer is to play the evaluation game by rules solely determined by the Customer; rules you may not know and that may not benefit you, the seller.

Your ability to jointly develop a plan with the buying team also serves as a strong indicator on whether the Customer will work with you effectively after the sale.

If an existing customer rejects your overtures to jointly set the buying rules for an upcoming new sale, it is a sure sign that you likely have to either invest more time in building the relationship. Or it may be time to decide that no matter what you do, this customer is simply not going to work with you collaboratively. It may be time to stop investing your company's valuable sales time and resources with this customer and move on to another potential customer.

While downgrading resources and time committed to an account is always a tough decision, sales professionals cannot sell to everyone and are better off focusing on customers with the highest potential.

19 – Quid Pro Quo is a key concept for staying in control of your time and resource investments with each client!

Decide early on how much time you will allocate across your accounts and how much time you are going to spend on each particular client. Equally important, determine how much time you are prepared to invest when you receive nothing in return.

Sales Thought: Quid pro quo is Latin for "this for that" and can help you balance your time and resource investment in each account.

In every sale there comes a point where you, the seller, have to decide how much time to invest in a particular customer and deal. Determining your time investment for each customer doesn't mean you will stop doing everything on the account, but that you will prioritize your time and stop doing non-priority things for the account. Smart sellers know that some customers will continue asking for more and more. If the seller keeps giving time and expertise for free, it's a natural reaction for the customer to keep asking!

The trick is having a rule for balancing and controlling customer requests within your selling time and resources.

Good sales people set up a quid pro quo understanding with buyers early in every Sales Process. This helps establish that your time, talent and resources are as valuable as the buyer's time. If the buyer is asking you to invest in the account, you should expect the buyer to tangibly move the Sales Process forward.

If this understanding is not established early in the buying cycle, the customer will keep asking and asking for investments of your time without reciprocation.

Not establishing a quid pro quo understanding in all your accounts almost guarantees that you, the seller, will be involved in a lot of sales cycles, but not necessarily in control of any. The lack of control will make your selling process chaotic and stressful for both you and your team.

Earlier in this book I made the comment that control in the sales cycle is an illusion. Establishing quid pro quo will minimize the chaos and maximize whatever control you can exert.

As a sales professional you have to determine how much time and resource you are going to invest in a particular sales cycle, for a particular Customer. Quid pro quo means that you will invest more in the sales cycle as long as you determine the Customer is investing. If a Customer is asking for more and more of your time during the sales cycle, at some point you have to decide whether the time is worth investing.

One technique that I often use, particularly in situations where a buyer or buying team keeps asking for more and more time from me, is to ask for access to a higher-level person in the account. This is a logical request. Clearly they are requesting answers from me to questions asked by someone else.

That is the only explanation for asking new questions. Asking for access the person behind the question is a way to speed up the process and stop wasting everyone's time – yours and theirs.

It is also a clear test for your relationship. The key is to ask for a quid pro quo at the right time, and not only at the beginning or end of the Sales Cycle:

- Ask Too Early: You have probably not earned the right yet
- Ask Too Late: Will have already done a lot of work in the Sales Cycle, and the Customer already thinks that you will keep "Doing Things" in hope of completing the Sales Cycle.

Sales Thought: You must demonstrate to the buyer that your time is just as valuable as theirs if you hope to have any semblance of control in the account.

Again, there are no absolutes. Sometimes you might feel you have a really good reason for "going along" with the customer as they go through their internal buying process and thus end up giving the account more time. However, if you find yourself investing a lot of selling "this" for very little "that" with the same customer, it is likely you have not established a quid pro quo relationship.

Sales Thought: If you don't have a quid pro quo understanding with the client, you are probably over-investing in the sale.

20 – In developing a sales account plan, realistically determine where you are today with each account before setting goals for the future.

Sales Account Planning often sparks a "self-abusing" tendency of sales people to include unrealistic objectives as part of the plan.

Example: I recently worked with a Sales Team that identified a particular large customer as being a strategic, long-term account of significant importance to the company's success for entering a new market space. The Sales Team had great intentions and ideas for managing the account strategically. They incongruously planned a quick first sale to the customer. I asked them if they thought it likely that this sales effort would happen quickly. They admitted it was not likely, particularly given that they were targeting this client as a market leader in a new market space and industry where they weren't currently selling.

In this case, it was important for the Sales Team to realistically acknowledge where they were with the account – objectively, nowhere. The situation at the time of setting the account plan was that they were "just another vendor" to the targeted client, and an unknown vendor at that. The Sales Team needed to acknowledge this fact in their goal setting for the client. The Team needed to build a plan that would realistically position them over time. The team had a common misperception, one I see in most sales people and Sales Teams: underestimating the time it takes to change a customer's perception of your offering. This can and does take a long time.

The Sales Team in this case must demonstrate behavior that convinces the customer of two very important things:

- The Sales Team must be willing to treat the customer as a Strategic Account with long-term objectives.
- The Sales Team must be willing to change its "selling behavior" to be more focused on long-term success for both the customer and the selling organization.

If your Sales Team is not prepared to take these two steps, you will likely have a hard time moving the needle when it comes to creating Strategic Accounts.

Sales Thought: Focus on the current state of the relationship. Until you acknowledge where you are today in the Customer Relationship, any and all planning you do is based on an incorrect assessment of your current relationship.

A great writer once said: "No matter what, when you want to go from Point A to Point B, first you have to acknowledge that you are where you are!"

Sales Thought: It's fine to say where you want to take the account relationship, but you must be realistic in acknowledging where you are with the account at the time you set your goals. Set your goals based on current realities!

21 – Goals-Objectives-Tactics-Actions: Tight linkage within the plan – top-down and bottom-up – is the best way to ensure successful sales.

Sales Planning is generally a skill that has to be developed by Sales Professionals. Not many sales people are blessed with planning as a natural skillset. By personality type, the Sales Professionals I work with typically have a "get it done now" personality type, focused on the other skills required by the Sales Profession. Sales actions are most often about getting things done to drive buying groups to a decision.

As one of my consulting friends often reminds me, "Our greatest strengths as professionals become our greatest weaknesses when we over-utilize them."

The problem with the strength of "getting things done" is that, if you plan to work with a customer long-term, you have to build a long-term plan.

Plans need to be top-down. The strategy that works for most teams is made up of:
- Goals
- Objectives
- Tactics or Actions

In my experience, Sales Teams tend to have an easier time building the Actions within the plan than other components. As they move to up to Objectives and Goals the Plan becomes a bit more confusing. The Build process works the best Top Down.

A Plan prevents Sales Teams from getting lost. A Plan helps the Sales Team understand how all the account activity ties together and leads to a defined outcome. By having a solid Plan, Sales Teams are in a better position to ensure the work the hard work going into each particular account will always lead towards the defined end game."

The key part of building the plan is to create linkage from top-to-bottom – from goals to actions.

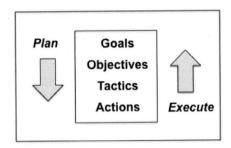

Sales Thought: You must focus on Planning from top-to-bottom.

22 – The test of a well-designed plan is that it enables you to execute from the bottom up – from Actions to Goals.

Sales Thought: You build the plan from the *top down*, but you execute the plan from the *bottom up*.

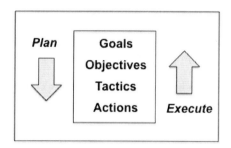

For Sales Plan Execution: Actions are linked to → **Tactics** are linked to → **Objectives** → are linked to → **Goals**

As you execute a specific action on behalf the account, consider how that action is linked to an upper-level tactic. If it's not linked, then why are you taking that particular action?

Sales Thought: There is a defining question you can use to determine whether you are effectively utilizing your Strategic Account plan. I separate true sales professionals from the people who "do things" by asking this linkage question:

"How is this action you are taking on behalf of the account linked to the plan?

If the answer to the linkage question is always:

"Because the prospect or customer asked me to."

Then, mission control, we have a problem.

Selling is a world of busy people who are constantly working with customers or prospects. To be successful in this chaotic profession, you have to execute against a real sales plan.

Building and executing useful and meaningful sales plans is a decision you make as a Sales Professional, or do not make. You can be as busy as you want, but if you don't take the time to plan, you will be continually executing things that are not strategic. At this point events would be driving your selling actions, not a thoughtful roadmap.

Example: Recently, a Sales Team I was coaching was working with a customer that began to ask for more and more resources, information, and presentations – Plan Activities – than were in the original Plan developed with the Customer. I asked them to look at the Plan and determine if either the Plan was not being followed, not properly written, or if the Customer had changed the jointly agreed to rules of the sale.

Once you recognize you are off Plan, it's time to decide if either the Plan needs to updated, and/or the Customer needs to be given a "Quid Pro Quo" test to see if they are really working with you in the process or they are simply making you and your team go through an exercise with no intention of buying.

This is a common example of where having a Plan can save lot of wasted effort. Having a Plan helps the Sale Team recognize they are off course a lot sooner than executing without one and can save valuable time and resources from being expended in a losing sales situation.

Executing without a plan is like running 2,600 100-meter dashes versus pacing yourself for a marathon.

23 – Your sales focus has to be continuous and consistent. Execute transactions within the framework of the overall Sales Strategy to stay on course!

There are many ways to sell - no question about it. The most interesting approach I see is by salespeople claiming to be strategic, but focusing instead on selling short-term deals. My experience is that it is very hard to be both strategic and short-term deal focused on the same account.

Sales Thought: Selling is a balancing act of having and executing an overall strategy built around long-term customer needs while working on account actions in a continuous and consistent manner.

- **Continuous:** You must work on building a relationship that stresses long-term continuity to the customer – indicating that it's not about this one project or one deal, but the long-term relationship.

- **Consistent:** You have to be sure that you don't get focused on any one aspect of the plan. Consistently focusing on all plan components that are important to the customer, not just the closing. Inconsistency can make you seem like ALL you care about is getting that deal done.

It's perfectly fine to have a goal of getting a deal done, but the customer is interested in your focus on a bigger picture that will result in a long-term relationship. Successful sales people continuously and consistently focus on an overall relationship that goes much further than one transaction.

Clearly you have a choice to make! If you focus on building the overall Customer Relationship while executing on a deal-by-deal basis, you will be better off in the long term.

Many sales situations may force the buyer and seller to make decisions about the relationship and where it is going. Depending on the situation that the seller and buyer find themselves in, there may be pressure to act in a different fashion. Based on much experience and many examples, it's usually better to be focused on the long run first. This behavior typically leads to more success from a relationship perspective. Nothing is perfect. However, the nature of selling may lead you down one path or another. From a big picture perspective, having the overall flow worked out is usually for the best.

Sales Thought: Having an overall strategy is one of the fundamentals of Sales Strategy. While you don't have to do anything, the nature of sales will require you to make a choice at some point.

Be continuous and consistent in how you work with your customers!

24 – At the beginning of each quarter, systematically provide a critical assessment (Stop/Start/Continue) on ALL planned sales activities for ALL accounts!

One of the most difficult things for sales people to do is to *stop doing* stuff. In most cases, sales people focus on "staying busy" and on activity. While activity is important, it can be very dangerous to find yourself in an activity mode, simply doing things without having an overall Game Plan in place.

Most good salespeople are very good at critically assessing themselves. They focus on determining what needs to be done for each account on a fairly continual basis. The reason that this is important is that, if you keep doing actions that are not connected to higher-level strategies, goals, or tactics, you end up with a finished a set of activities. But you may still find yourself asking an embarrassing question:

"Why did I just do all of those things for this Customer/Account/Opportunity?"

Sales Thought: The most important thing you can do as a Sales Professional is to take stock of each account on a quarterly basis.

Quarterly, ask yourself the following three questions:

1. "Of the activities I am doing today, which ones should I keep doing" (Continue)?
2. "Which activities do I stop doing?" (Stop) This is probably the hardest category!
3. "What new activities do I need to add to my list?" (Start)

The most difficult answer to the above questions is to stop doing something where you may have already invested a lot of time and energy. If you are not getting any return on the investment of time, STOP investing!

Sales Thought: Ensure you do a regular, honest evaluation of each account. Also, make sure you are investing in activities that will lead to further expansion of your business with each customer!

THREE -- PENETRATING AND MANAGING ACCOUNTS

Penetrating and Managing Accounts

The need for penetrating and managing accounts depends on the specific type of sales job you have. While requirements for developing sales techniques vary by job, these skills round out a sales professional's ability and marketability!

Many sales jobs are based on the pure "hunter" model - finding new accounts and getting customers to buy. What happens after the sale is generally someone else's problem. However, more and more sales roles are becoming focused on the notion of "hunting and farming." The farming role involves cultivating clients for the long-term by growing the size and profitability of the accounts. Therefore the "hunting and farming" role places a great deal of value on the style you use to penetrate the account and make the sale.

Hunting and farming requires the ability to focus selling *more* to the same customers. This requires the sales person to wear multiple "hats" of both hunter and farmer. If you have to do both, or are interested in expanding your sales skills and marketability, the information in this section is for you!

1 – Effective sales professionals DON'T feel the need to carry every customer conversation. You will be more effective when you don't take this approach.

So many people in sales seem to think it is important for them to talk about what they are selling. The issue with this "my product is important" mindset (and the accompanying sales pitch) is that both reinforce the buyer's opinion of you as "just another sales person."

Sales Thought: True sales professionals find the right mix of talking and listening in each selling situation.

Most great sales people focus on upfront learning about each potential customer's needs. This occurs during the opening conversation. While your initial goal should be to go through "classic" discovery, more and more, clients are expecting sales people to come in being more prescriptive. Now, it certainly depends on who you are representing, but many clients won't give you the time to go through a lot of Discovery until you have earned the right to go through it.

As such, many sales professionals have to go through the process of demonstrating that they understand the customer walking in to the situation. It is not about knowing all about the customer, but it is about being able to start out by saying:

"We have helped a variety of organizations in similar situations address a variety of business needs, including X, Y, and Z."

The customer should see that you walk with a high level understanding of their business. The most common question from the Customer tends to be "What do you want from us?"

A classic answer would be:

"We would like to know how you are addressing X, Y, and Z today and provide you with examples of how we have assisting other clients address these issues."

If starting from the beginning, your initial goal for the sales conversation is to discover what this particular customer wants and needs. Listen for what your customers think they are looking for. Each customer has given this some thought before you arrived. You won't find anything out if you are doing all the talking. Resist the urge to break the ice by talking about what your product does. Listen first! Incorporate what you learn from customers about their needs before you start selling.

Sales Thought: Match your sales pitch to the customer's business need by listening before selling.

The right mix of talking and listening is typically a combination of:

- Discovery questions that allow you to learn more about the customer, the account, and the deal at hand
- Follow-up questions that probe into the customer's needs
- Statements about your understanding of the problem, followed by a question: "Did I get that right?"
- Then, selling into the agreed-upon problems.

It's critical to be mindful of the amount of time you are talking versus the amount of time the customer is talking.

Example: I was working with a particular sales person who indicated that she was struggling to break into some accounts. She indicated that she had done a number of presentations of her products, but nothing was happening as a result. I suggested that, instead of presenting her product, she could start her meetings out with a list of questions for each and every meeting. I suggested she take the answers and then come back for a follow-up presentation. After doing this, she was able to break into a number of new accounts and had totally changed her sales approach to listen first before making any presentations!

2 – Whether you know it or not, you earn the right to speak and to be listened to by your customers.

Think about this example… You arrive at a sales conference for a little networking. Soon you strike up a conversation with a rep from a company you'd like to learn about. She talks for about 15 minutes about their new killer product line, why she came to the conference, sales prospects she is pursuing, why her products are so good and how sales are booming. You patiently nod your head and listen. Meanwhile you are learning a lot, although you are waiting your turn to talk. When she stops for oxygen, you finally get to interject your name and company. She says, "Oh great. Can you get me in to see it and the right person to purchase my product?" You give her the name of the right person. She says thanks and walks off to her next "presentation" victim.

How do you feel when on the receiving end of a conversation like this? When you entered the hypothetical conversation you expected give and take. You planned to be part of a dialogue.

Now ask yourself, honestly, does your customer get a similar impression of you after your sales call? Does your sales call leave the customer feeling like it's a one-way street with you and your product the center of attention? If so, you are in trouble.

I frequently observe sales people delivering a one-way conversation where the customer is left feeling like a victim of "drive-buy" selling.

Sales Thought: Your customers expect you to listen. They expect to tell you about their business problems and that you will address them.

Anything less than focused listening will be viewed by them as not caring, and a one-sided interaction.

Sales Tactic: Become comfortable talking less and listening more.

Find a balance between listening versus talking. It needs to work for you and your style. My guess is that the balance you currently have may be talk-heavy and listen-light.

I work on this balance regularly. I just pick one call each week to focus on how much I am talking versus listening. (Without actively and regularly measuring myself, I would not be conscious of my personal ratio of talk versus listen.)

To be great in sales, one must learn the proper balance between talking and listening. The goal should be to create a productive, problem-focused dialogue with the customer. If you can, then you have started a professional conversation – one with some prospect of advancing the business relationship.

Sale Tactic: Avoid the temptation that affects so many sales people: the need to pitch product.

The moment you start talking – pitching product – without first listening, you have become merely a sales person, and you reinforce all of the customer's stereotypes about sales people.

Sales Thought: Carrying on a two-way conversation is the most effective way to show that you have the ability to listen and ask good questions!

Sales Thought: Become comfortable, over time, talking less.

Learning a proper balance that works for you and your style is key.

Sales professionals learn the proper balance between asking questions and creating a realistic dialogue with the customer.

Starting and maintaining professional sales conversation is a critical skill. If you can create a fluid selling conversation with the buyer, you have taken the first step in avoiding the temptation that affects so many sales people – the need to pitch product.

Sales Thought: The moment you start pitching product, you have become another "sales person," and you are only reinforcing all of the stereotypes that are out there about every sales person!

Sales Thought: Not dominating a conversation demonstrates to the customer that you might lack the ability to listen.

3 – To expand your presence in an account, don't repeat the same messages and just keep talking to the same people. Change your "Angle of Attack!"

It's not good enough to focus your attention on the same people over and over again. You have heard the old adage - doing the same things and expecting different results is the definition of insanity.

Once the buyer makes it clear there is "no opportunity" at an account, you should work with your management team to determine if you can afford to walk away from the account. If your leadership deems it necessary to proceed with the account and make additional investment of time, talent and resources, the next set of questions that your organization must ask are:

- "To whom at the account have we recently spoken?"
- "Have we talked to any new contacts at this account recently?"
- "What products or services have we tried to position at the account?"

There are two areas you should review and pursue if you are determined to move forward with a "no opportunity" account.

- **New People:** Find new people to talk with. Sales people often spend their time with the same people and hit them over and over again. It gets annoying for the people involved and boringly unproductive for the sales person.

- **New Message:** Position yourself differently with a different message. Positioning is all about having a message that will resonate with the person you are talking to.

So, how should you proceed?

I call this the *"new people/new message approach"* to changing the angle of attack. The big idea is that you change the person or change the message. In some cases, it takes both to have a new approach. You can't just keep saying the same thing to the same person over and over again!

Sales Thought: Successful sales people will always continue to expand their presence by finding new ways to enlarge and expand their client contact points.

Sales Thought: Sometimes the "new person" might need you to ask for a new person from your account team to become engaged in the account.

4 – Don't overly focus on the next deal. Work to expand relationships in an account by engaging all the members of your sales team with the key people at the account!

If you only focus on the next deal, you will eventually wear out your welcome at the account. If you instead focus on expanding and engaging new relationships, you will become valuable to the client. It's clearly a choice you make, but consider it carefully.

Think about it this way:

- **Deal-Focused:** This Option is only about selling. It's hard to show the customer you care about them if you only talk with them when there's a deal on the table. Ultimately it's your call, but you can't have it both ways. You can't build a relationship when all you care about is the next deal!

- **Relationship-Focused:** In this case, you are willing and ready to engage with the customer when there is no deal on the table. You show that you are focused on them and that they matter. It also demonstrates that you are focused on a long-term relationship.

One approach is not necessarily better than another. The approach you take is a matter of choice. Having both choices in your tool-kit and determining the right choice is key.

Your choice of approach depends on a number of factors. The following factors can be used to determine your choice for how you engage.

Reasons to focus *short-term* include:

- Your compensation is based only on closing current deals.
- The account doesn't want a relationship with you.
- You are dealing with lower-level people on the customer side who only focus on current deals.

Reasons to focus on a *long-term* relationship include:

- Demonstrating you are interested in the client, not just on the next deal.
- Getting a chance to come back and to sell some other product or service to them later.
- Getting access to more high-level people.

Many sales people are successful doing their job one way or another. It simply comes down to preference. In some cases, it is company philosophy. In some cases, senior management tells the sales team how they want them to engage with each customer. It comes down to a matter of selecting an approach, for you and for your company.

Sales Thought: Be aware of these sales framing options as you sell. Don't' be afraid to use the appropriate options and vary their use by account and circumstance.

5 – Focus is critical for sales teams. Don't buy into wild changes of direction. Stay focused on the big picture!

Consistent execution is key to sales success. I have noticed that companies often make changes to sales strategy when they think it will rapidly improve sales. Actually, when you make major sales strategy changes the sales team is forced to adjust everything they have put in place with their customers. Everyone, you and the customer, can lose in these situations. The impacts for each are:

- **Sales Company:** The sales company loses credibility with frequent changes to sales strategy because the changes typically confuse your employees more than helping to make them more successful. No one likes change, except a wet baby. The sales team blames your company for creating confusion and uncertainty. Some sales people leave the company when this occurs, for they want to find a place that is more stable.

- **Sales Teams:** Changes to sales strategy can look bad to customers. The Sales Team looks like they don't know what they are doing when they keep approaching customers with ever-changing messages.

- **Customers:** Customers don't want to work with companies that are continuingly changing the rules of engagement. They get nervous and antsy. Continually changing selling direction complicates the buying decision and often engenders doubt about your company's stability and direction. Doubt is not good for closing.

So, you can't continuously change strategy. Therefore you need to set an "A" Strategy and manage towards it. If you continuously change strategies, you end up confusing the customer and making your sales force uneasy.

While some changes due to the introduction of game changing products or offerings (or by the competition!) are inevitable, these are relatively rare events in any marketplace. It is better to continue positioning what you have today, maintaining consistency in the eyes of the customers, rather than introducing a change of strategy. Be focused on the big picture that your customers care about. They most certainly don't care about your new strategic approach unless you give them a good reason – a game-changing reason.

Example: In working with one organization, I found they were given continually changing product direction. The head of sales finally decided, "Enough is enough!" and told the sales team to "stay the course" for the coming quarter. The sales team held the course and sales for that quarter increased by 20%. Customers who had previously been very confused were much more assured about the stability and certainty of their supplier. It was a breakthrough that really changed how the company did business going forward.

Changing strategy will likely confuse customers, inject unfounded uncertainty into the relationship, and do more harm than good!

Sales Thought: You can't have an ever-changing strategy. Instead you must focus on a consistent overall strategy for each account. Stay focused on the big picture with each customer.

6 – Take a step back from your sales opportunity to be sure you REALLY understand the customer's needs.

One of the most difficult things for a sales person is NOT to sell. When you face a situation where you are forced to position your product, there is a natural tendency to "pitch" the product. While this may seem necessary to move the sale forward, you usually end up doing yourself a lot of harm when you pitch too early.

When you are not sure of the situation with your client, take a step back and focus on understanding the customer's "real need." There is a reason they are asking these questions. You need to understand that reason. This is critical to moving forward with the sale. If you don't take the time to understand the reasons, you are likely to find yourself throwing things against the wall and hoping something sticks. This is not a good place for sales professionals. Being there involves high pressure on you and is a sure sign you are failing with the customer.

While you may have occasional success pitching ideas on the fly, it puts you in the same category as less-skilled sales people. When you perceive you are in this situation, instead of talking about your product, take some time to ensure that you understand the customer's real need or concern. The only way forward is to ask your customer some probing questions to see what is driving the pressure you feel.

Sales Thought: Don't pitch when you fall under pressure; ask questions – particularly when you feel stuck.

Skillful probing of your customer's root concern, and establishing a conversational dialogue about their real needs or concerns, may seem to be a counter-intuitive response. The pressure you feel in the sales situation should be an indication that you have not established rapport with the customer and that they have concerns or issues.

Without a better understanding of the customer's concerns or issues, moving forward with a sales pitch is high risk, at best. Make it your intuitive action, when you feel under pressure, to get a better understanding of what the customer is trying to accomplish and why. Internalizing this sales tactic will ensure that, when you do start talking about your product, you do it with a clearer understanding of the points you need to cover.

Without knowledge of what the customer is really looking for, you cannot address the customer's needs. The added benefit of internalizing this approach is that questioning under pressure gives you information on how to target your product. You will also have a better opportunity to distinguish yourself from other sales people who immediately start talking about their product.

By showing that you really care about and understand the "real need," you have the chance to position your product in a way that "really" fits the customer.

Sales Thought: When you feel pressure in a selling situation, you probably are not addressing or understanding what the customer is looking for.

Taking time to capture customer need is the single most important thing a sales person should focus on during a pressure moment. If you don't understand real need, you can't position your sales effort to address the real problems!

7 – If you are not demonstrating "Win-Win" with your sales approach, don't expect the customer to be a partner in the selling process! Win-Win matters and results in long term profitable deals!

Admittedly, the sales process makes it easy to create a winner and a loser in every selling event. Many people believe that every sale results in a winner and a loser. While this belief may be true about some specific situations, sales processes that produce winners and losers are not healthy for a long-term relationship. Customers have likely experienced a previous sales process where they felt like the loser. Thus, sales people often feel like they have lost even when they make the sale. Naturally, customers who have been burned in the past by sales people are working hard to win this time. Defining a credible win-win approach to selling and working with your customer to implement this approach is healthier and less stressful for both parties.

I recommend that all sales professionals become convinced that sales can yield a win-win outcome and that they start every sale looking for the possibility that there be no losers. Adopting this approach and selling philosophy allows you to act in an honorable fashion and benefits you, your company, and your customer.

Example: Customers react to being sold to by putting in place new process for future buys. This is feedback to the Seller that they were unhappy with the Buying experience. A bad Buying experience can lead Customers to implement a request for proposal (RFP) process instead of an ongoing dialogue. In this situation the sales person may wonder why this has happened, when it was likely driven by a win-lose seller.

Adopting a win-win sales approach also allows you to think about a longer-term relationship with the customer and gives you a better shot at working with each customer through multiple sales cycles.

Sales Thought: Customers that feel like losers will not be repeat customers.

133

I'm always amazed at the number of sales people approaching each customer for a sales win, but not caring about the customer's sense of getting a win. These same sales people are always shocked when the customer will not consider another sales cycle. Often customers avoid the next round of Win-Lose selling by setting up the rules so the sales person loses all future rounds or loses their business.

When you start down a path of win-win selling, you approach each customer with the following thoughts:

- Both sides can win and benefit from the deal.
- The relationship is a long-term one, worth the investment.
- We will both want to do more business together in the future.

Approaching the sales process with these philosophies allows you to be much more successful in the long run!

Sales Thought: If you focus on winning at the expense of your customer, your customer will turn on you and ultimately put you in the position of losing out.

Win-Lose selling is a short-term phenomenon. If customers feel like losers, they will want to get even. Focusing on win-win is the only way to go in long-term relationships.

8 – Prospecting is a combination of having the right Message and consistently repeating it. You need to master both!

Almost daily I find myself in discussions about prospecting. Most sales people really don't get it. Let me break the code for you: Unless you have game-changing product or service, selling is always, to some degree, a numbers game. Therefore you must have a large population of potential prospects that you reach out to. Of those you reach, only a percentage of them will be true prospects for what you sell. More prospecting leads to more true selling opportunities. More *effective* prospecting equals more sales.

The really interesting question I ask sales professionals is:

"What do you do when you have found a true prospect?"

The answer to this question is, in part, what separates great sales people from the merely good ones. Sales professionals grasp that the key to turning prospects into sales is getting the potential customer to think your way about your product, and to do this quickly and consistently.

There are two parts to prospecting that will really help you focus prospects on thinking why your product is the answer.

The right message about your product: It's not a pure "feature-function" discussion. It's about how you go about positioning your product that separates you from the other sales people. It needs to be a thoughtful message. And it must quickly position the benefits for the customer. The right message is hard to craft. Messages are not completely generic, but actually require slight adjustment for each prospect based on your insight.

Sales Thought: You must have a *consistently repeated message* for each account.

Unfortunately, most sales people change messages each time they call on the prospect. This not only doesn't work, it confuses the prospect and reinforces stereotypical feelings about you as a sales person. Neither of these outcomes, confusion or your appearance as a typical sales person, will lead to a good result.

Instead of delivering mixed messages, ensure that you settle on a key message quickly, and then repeat it. If the prospect enters the selling process by hearing a key message, one that makes sense for them, and you repeat the Message to multiple prospects within the account, this will become your Message.

Think of this as water dripping on a rock. When you drop it the first time, it bounces. If you keep up the drip – with the right delivery – it will begin to have an impact!

Sales Thought: The combination of right Message and consistency will help you get true prospects into the selling process.

9 – In writing sales-call-plans for customer meetings, the key element is simple: craft great questions!

Far too many sales people start the first customer meeting by focusing on their products. They seem to think that everyone who agrees to meet with them wants to hear about product features and functions. Let me assure you that potential prospects did not agree to meet with you just to listen to this. Interestingly enough, talking about features and functions on the first call is the exact opposite of what real sales pros do. The better sales professionals come to the first meeting with a customer or prospect and focus on learning about the prospect.

Sales Thought: What is the best way to learn? Not by talking, but by asking great questions!

OK, now that you understand the need to design your first meeting with the prospect differently – from presenting features and functions to asking questions to learn – you may be surprised that it's still not enough. There is one additional focus point. You have to craft and ask the right type of questions. The best questions are open-ended questions.

What is an open-ended question? The prospect's answer to an open-ended question cannot be yes or no. (Yes or no answers define the opposite type - closed-ended questions. Closed-ended questions are great for closing, but not for early prospect meetings.)

Sales Tactic: Open-ended questions demand more detailed answers and consequently provide more information.

What great sales people do is to continually ask these types of questions to prompt a conversation. By prompting a conversation, you are continually learning more about your customer or prospect. There is plenty of time to sell and talk about features and functions and there will be opportunities to make these points later on.

Craft your early-stage prospect meeting plans with a focus on open-ended questions. You will quickly learn what you need to know to move the sale forward. Open-ended questions help you uncover and learn the why and how of what the customer wants to accomplish. Learning the why and how allows you to more effectively introduce the relevant capabilities of your product.

Open-ended questions provide you the ammo and targets for later demonstration of how your product or service specifically addresses the client's stated needs/solves their problems. Answers to open-ended questions provide the learning you need to address the why and the how of what the customer is looking for and wants to accomplish.

Asking why and how questions, you will be much better prepared to tie what you are offering to what the customer needs.

Sales Thought: Not preparing a meeting plan means that you have decided to go into the meeting without a plan. Face it; in that case you are not really prepared to sell.

Remember, there is *always* enough time to create a few great open-ended questions.

10 – Rapid execution of an 80% complete sales plan is better than waiting for 100% of the information to be available before executing. Rapid execution is everything.

I consistently see sales teams slowing down by seeking too much information before executing a sales plan. They have the mistaken idea that they need to have perfect information to be perfect on execution. Perfect execution should not be a goal. Perfect execution is a standard of excellence to strive for. But this standard can rarely if ever be attained, particularly in complex sales.

Finding a balance in the level of information in the plan takes time. Focus on the covering the big stuff and don't sweat the smaller details.

Sales Thought: Without perfect information, perfect execution is impossible.

I have worked with sales teams that were overly focused on perfection. I often point out that relevant account information changes at a blinding pace. Consequently, it's harder and harder to execute flawlessly. As such, sales teams sometimes feel stuck and unable to move forward because they don't have all the information. Once again, if you don't have perfect information, you cannot be perfect in your execution. Execution rules need to be revised.

In developing each part of the sales plan, focus on having reasonable, but not necessarily perfect, information. As a benchmark, try for around 80% of the necessary information to complete the plan. This will be painful for highly analytic members of the sales team. With 80% of the information in hand, you should be able to execute the plan. While executing, always look to acquire the missing 20%, but never wait for it.

This 80% reality leads you to the following guidelines:

- Rapid execution of an 80% complete sales plan is a better course of action than waiting for more information.
- You will never have 100% of the information you need for sales planning.

Speed is the key. You will make some mistakes. When you do, correct the mistake and move on. The 80% approach will make you more effective in working with most customers. While customers judge sales people on multiple criteria, rapid execution is one of the primary factors. Getting the customer to a point where they can make the best decision possible is going to bring you the most success in the long run.

Sales Thought: In today's selling environment, you cannot fixate on being perfect (though this should be the ideal goal). You will make mistakes along the way. The key is to make the mistakes fast and then make corrections!

11 – Account planning, done correctly, is hard work. Developing account plans that make you successful doesn't happen overnight.

Change your focus from simply selling more to selling more - profitably. It's true that some product sales require that you just sell more. It does depend on what you sell. Truly accomplished sales people take on a variety of activities that will help them be successful with a particular account - not just in the short run, but also for the long haul. The real question for a sales people is not "selling more." It's making the moves to make the sale:

- **Profitable** – Because otherwise your company cannot afford to consistently do business this way!
- **Win-Win** – Good for both sides – because true sales professionals focus on true "win-win." Otherwise, the sales cycle is typically not repeatable!

To achieve win-win selling: What is often lacking is something that sounds simple. But, if done correctly, it's not easy at all:

Sales Thought: A repeatable account plan covers a wide variety of areas of interest, and focuses on being good for all parties.

Account planning is not easy if done correctly. This is because there are many factors to take into consideration, and many sales people do not have the patience to truly "plan." Account planning is a learned process. Without good oversight, many sales people become shortsighted and just focus on "the next deal." You can do this, but it's unlikely that this account will be profitable for you!

Sales Thought: What most sales teams need to improve on is emphasis on building the plan! Creating a profitable account is based on having a "real" strategy and that requires a PLAN.

12 – Relationship management is better executed when there ISN'T an active deal. Invest a little time, all the time, for long-term success.

Too many sales people only engage when there is a deal on the table. The problem here is that, if you engage the customer only during the active sales cycles, you will miss selling opportunities in the 95% of your clients who may not be active right now.

Another consequence of only working with customers during the selling cycle is losing track of ongoing issues and personnel changes in the account. Also, you will be missing out on emerging threats and opportunities. Long-term working relationships with customers require you to demonstrate an on-going commitment. It really doesn't take that much effort to implement this concept. A small investment of time and attention will signal to the customer that you are interested in them - not just now, but for the long run!

Too many people in sales do not engage the customer outside of the active sales cycle. The argument I most often hear is "There is no deal on the table." The problem is, if you don't engage with a customer on a consistent basis, you may not find out about the next deal or a competitor's move to steal your account. It's your choice. However, trusted business advisors maintain regular contract with their customers whether there is business on the table or not.

One last thought on the nature of customer engagement: If there is nothing active on the table, it is the ideal time to engage the customer. When there is an active deal, communication between buyer and seller is usually focused only on the deal. If there is not a deal, it's the ideal time to improve and develop relationships. This is the time when customers openly communicate about needs and problems. Why? With nothing on the table, there is no reason for the customer to hide things from the seller. You will be able to learn about upcoming projects and that will set up the relationship to be very collaborative.

Sales Thought: The reality is that, if you want real respect from a customer, don't be a "hit and run" seller. Focus your attention on them when there is nothing on the table. That will help you achieve Trusted Business Advisor status.

Depending on how your Company goes to market, you will have decisions to make along the way. Historically, focusing on the big picture is the territory of the Trusted Business Advisor. It is harder and will consume more time. But, in the long run, you will be a better seller and your customer will have a reason to continue to engage with you.

Final Thoughts on <u>Sales Thoughts</u>, Circa 2014

There are a lot of books on Sales in the market. This is not an attempt to write yet another one that summarizes the same way, and leaves you wondering.

The most important lessons I try to focus on here are the following:

- It's Not "Always Be Closing" it is "Always Be Learning." The moment a Great Seller stops learning, they stop being a Great Seller. It is about being continually aware of what is going on in the market and adapting.
- Focus on Process First: Great Sellers are Process Experts. Each Element that is covered in this book is designed to be Part of an overall Process. Depending on what you do and what you sell, the importance of each section can be debated. What is not up for debate is that it is all a part of a Process
- Learn to ask Good Questions: Learning this one skill will help you become a MUCH better Seller. If you don't do this, then you will have difficulty internalizing the rest of the Process.
- Learn to work in a Team Environment: Great Sellers are Team Players, not Commandos. Work within a team Environment, and you will be better off in the long run.
- Play for the Long Run: Great Sellers are focused on working an Account from a Long Term, Win-Win perspective. Getting a deal here or a deal there does not make a great seller. Learning how to execute and repeat is what matters!
- Win-Win is Key: If you don't focus on this, it is only a matter of time before it comes back to haunt you! You may win a deal here or a deal there, but great sellers believe in this very important concept!
- Whatever you sell, "Pitching Your Product" is a bad idea. In this day and age, it is only a matter of time before the next "Great" Mouse trap comes along.
- Don't get focused on Product Features and Functions- or else you run the risk of being a Product Seller. The next thing that will happen is you will start Pitching, and the Customer reaction will be "I've Seen that already." You will be Pitching "Better Sameness" in your presentation, which leaves you open to being very much marginalized!

These items wind their way through all that is here, and we usually find a way to tie the key point back to one or more of these items!

Sales is a never ending, and ever changing set of skills. This book has tried to provide you with up to date skills that will help you approach Selling in the most up to date fashion possible.

The intent was and is to let you know where the "Art" of Salesmanship is circa 2014. As sure as I am writing this, there will be a continual Evolution in the Art. The most important thing that I have communicated here is that the best approach is to take each situation as an opportunity to expand your Learning. Whether it is about a Product, Customer Needs, Relationship Management, or a combination of all, the idea is that as you "Continually" Learn, you will be better able to work with each new client as you start the Sales Process.

What this was not designed to be was any kind of "Magic" bullet. There is no such thing. Those Sales People that have achieved Trusted Advisor Status have done so through the Art of Continually Learning and Continually Evolving their Sales approach. It is the appropriate combination if learning and positioning makes the true Sales Professional successful.

Keep looking for Sales Thoughts via Twitter or Facebook, or email. Our commitment to the Reader is that you will get continual updates based on continual learning.

We look forward to engaging with you as the World of Sales continues to evolve.

ABOUT THE AUTHORS

Phil Bush has gone down two Parallel tracks in his working career. With over 25 years of experience in Sales, Sales Management, Alliances and Channel Marketing, Bush has been very successful handling a wide variety of assignments in the area of Sales, Sales Management, Business Development, Channels, and Strategic Alliances.

Phil has spent the last several years focused on the combination of Strategic Account Planning and Sales Performance Coaching for multiple Divisions of IBM and Oracle. The focus was to drive revenue for different parts of the organizations. Bush continues to focus on the big picture of Sales and Sales Performance as a way to improve revenue attainment

Prior to this time, Phil served as Senior Principal for Atlanta-based Infomentis. Infomentis focused on expanding revenue streams for its clients in all areas, including Sales, Channels/Alliances, Services and Maintenance. Infomentis was in business for 14 years prior to being merged with the TAS Group. The High Tech Client List included Microsoft, Computer Associates, Cognos (purchased by IBM), Informatica, NetApp, and other High Tech companies. In his 6 years there, Bush started and developed the Sales Performance Coaching practice for Infomentis, focusing on helping each client's Sales Management and Sales Team execute individual sales activities, Strategic Planning, Territory Planning, and Sales Management techniques. This work has taken Bush around the world in helping sales teams improve their sales success, in some cases by as much as 50% in just under a year.

Previously, his focus ranged from start-ups, including work in the late 1990's at NEON (New Era of Networks) where he helped the Enterprise Application Integration (EAI) company go from $20 to $160 million in Revenue in near record fashion. From 2001 through 2005, Phil worked on a combination rebuilding/expansion assignment at Swedish-owned Telelogic (Purchased in 2008 by IBM,) a provider of Application Development Tools. As Senior Vice President of Global Strategic Accounts, he rebuilt the Strategic

Account Team into a formidable group response for $40M in revenue annually, and helped expand Strategic Account Selling and Development philosophies in the Asia-Pacific Area. He also established the first Global Alliances Program, including work with Technology Partners, Resellers, Channels and Referral Partners.

Earlier assignments including work in the ERP/MRP arena, GroupWare, and earlier versions of Application Development or CASE Tools.

Throughout his career, Bush has devised multiple sales and marketing methodologies with a focus on execution success. He has put together strategies and philosophies for almost every selling situation, particularly those focused on building easy-to-use selling processes. He continues to focus on reinforcement in the areas of Sales Methodologies, Repeatable Process, and Consistency of Delivery within each Sales Organization.

Phil's other area of Expertise is in and around Sports:
Phil Bush has been around and active in Sports for over 25 years. Whether as a player, Coach, Tournament Director, Producer, or Commentator, Phil has been on all sides of sports for a long time.

Bush currently is a Color Analyst for FSN South, CSS, ESPNU, and other networks, lending his expertise to volleyball broadcasts of Southeastern Conference (SEC) and the Atlantic Coast Conference (ACC). He also has become one of the "Voices" of International Volleyball working for the International Volleyball Federation (FIVB.) This has taken Phil to 17 countries broadcasting International Competition featuring teams from around the world both Indoors and on the Beach.

Bush has experience in other sports and roles: Phil previously handled sideline reporting duties for the Georgia Tech Radio Football Network, and was involved with the Georgia Tech Basketball Network for over 5 years. He also has covered other events, such as track and field, soccer, and cross-country.

Bush's specialty is creativity in bringing the broadcast home to viewers by providing comparisons to other sports and asking questions to help bring the game closer to fans.

Bush also served as a Technical Supervisor and Television Coordinator for the International Volleyball Federation (FIVB.) In the role of Technical Supervisor, Phil traveled to Beach and Indoor Volleyball events around the world, overseeing Television Production for a variety of events. In the role of Television Coordinator, Phil worked with various Broadcast networks around the world to ensure that their Broadcasts are done in accordance with the policies of the FIVB.

Bush handled Event Production for Volleyball at the 1996 Olympics in Atlanta. This role was new to the Olympics, and involved coordinating and executing a plan to present the sport in the most positive way possible to the spectators in the live audience. Through the use of announcers, music, lights, effects, matrix boards and coordination of all those involved in the execution of the sport, Sports Production had never been formally done at the Olympics until 1996. Bush was the first Sports Producer hired by the Atlanta Organizing Committee, and helped define the role. The Production work was given rave reviews by the International Volleyball Federation, which declared that the Atlanta Olympics was the best ever in the presentation of the sport.

Phil also handles Traffic Coordinator Responsibilities for the world's largest 10K, The Peachtree Road Race. Here he coordinates a group of several hundred volunteers to assure that 60,000 runners can get where they are supposed to go with no interference from traffic, as well as assure that key vehicles that do need to get through can do so as needed.

Bush also ran Professional Beach Volleyball Tournaments in the 1980's, including the first ever Pro Tournaments in Florida, Arizona, and New York from 1982-85. From 1983-86, he ran the first ever "Satellite" Pro Beach Tour in Florida (sponsored by Tropical Blend) that covered 12 cities in Florida. This tour pioneered the "Regional"

Tour idea that has been duplicated many times since by other companies.

Because of his varied background in sports, he brings keen insight into the tactics, strategy, and adjustments implemented by teams. Phil's approach is particularly adept at helping viewers who might not know the sport well learn it as they watch the action. This "high energy" approach to broadcasting is one that has proven to be a great asset in translating the excitement of the sport to the broadcast audience.

Phil is a graduate of Georgia Tech. He resides in Atlanta with his wife Anna – Head Volleyball Coach and Assistant Athletic Director at Pace Academy, and 18-year-old daughter, Cory, a freshman in Music Theatre at NYU.

Brett Boston is the founder and president of Group Solutions®. He is an internationally recognized pioneer in the use of innovative processes for team-based collaborative technologies for creating complex business and market strategies. Brett has built and implemented strategies for over 100 of the Fortune 500, federal and state government agencies, the military, and non-profits. Brett has built strategies in 37 countries for global clients.

Brett brings vision, energy and a highly strategic level of thinking to any project. He is considered the leading electronic meeting facilitator in the world.

Brett is also the Executive Director of the Wildlife Foundation of Florida and is passionate about taking care of Florida's fish wildlife, and natural habitats for current and future generations.

Brett is a graduate of Emory University.